PHalarope Books are designed specifically for the amateur naturalist. These volumes represent excellence in natural history publishing. Most books in the PHalarope series are based on a nature course or program at the college or adult education level or are sponsored by a museum or nature center. Each PHalarope book reflects the author's teaching ability as well as writing ability. Among the books:

The Amateur Naturalist's Handbook
Vinson Brown

The Art of Field Sketching
Clare Walker Leslie

Biography of a Planet: Geology, Astronomy, and the Evolution of Life on Earth
Chet Raymo

The Curious Naturalist
John Mitchell and the Massachusetts Audubon Society

A Field Guide to the Familiar: Learning to Observe the Natural World
Gale Lawrence

A Natural History Notebook of North American Animals
National Museum of Natural History, Canada

Nature Drawing: A Tool for Learning
Clare Walker Leslie

Nature with Children of All Ages: Activities and Adventures for Exploring, Learning, and Enjoying the World Around Us
Edith A. Sisson

Pond and Brook: A Guide to Nature Study in Freshwater Environments
Michael J. Caduto

The Seaside Naturalist: A Guide to Nature Study at the Seashore
Deborah A. Coulombe

The Sky Observer's Guidebook
Charles E. Roth

Suburban Geology: An Introduction to the Common Rocks and Minerals of Your Back Yard and Local Park
Richard Headstrom

Suburban Wildflowers: An Introduction to the Common Wildflowers of Your Back Yard and Local Park
Richard Headstrom

Suburban Wildlife: An Introduction to the Common Animals of Your Back Yard and Local Park
Richard Headstrom

Thoreau's Method: A Handbook for Nature Study
David Pepi

365 Starry Nights: An Introduction to Astronomy for Every Night of the Year
Chet Raymo

MEMORIES FROM A NATURALIST'S NOTEBOOK

A YEAR OF FAVORITE OBSERVATIONS IN THE WORLD OF NATURE

by
Richard Headstrom

Illustrations & Commentary by
Carol Decker

PHalarope Books

Prentice Hall Press • New York

Text Copyright © 1986 by the Estate of Richard Headstrom, and Carol Decker
Illustrations Copyright © 1986 by Carol Decker
All rights reserved,
including the right of reproduction
in whole or in part in any form.

Published by Prentice Hall Press
A Division of Simon & Schuster, Inc.

PRENTICE HALL PRESS is a trademark of Simon & Schuster, Inc.

A PHalarope Book

Library of Congress Cataloging-in-Publication Data

Headstrom, Richard, 1902-
   Memories from a naturalist's notebook.

   Includes index.
   1. Natural history—Addresses, essays, lectures.
I. Decker, Carol. II. Title.
QH81.H39   1986   508   85-30150
ISBN 0-13-574377-X

Manufactured in the United States of America.

10 9 8 7 6 5 4 3 2 1

CONTENTS

FOREWORD   *vii*

WINTER   1

January 3   Bobcat 12
January 12   Blue Jay 15
January 19   Junco 19
January 26   Insect 23
February 5   Shrew 28
February 10   Kinglet 32
February 21   Mourning Cloak Butterfly 35
March 5   Hepatica 37
March 13   Grackle 40
March 16   Spring Azure Butterfly 42
March 22   Bumblebee 46
March 28   Ladybug 49

SPRING   53

April 1   Frog 61
April 5   Jack-in-the-Pulpit 69
April 7   Shadblow Tree 72
April 12   Elm 74
April 17   Dandelion 77
April 20   Grass 80
May 5   Peppermint 83
May 13   Buttercup 87
May 24   Sunfish 90
May 30   Orchid 94
June 1   Snake 98
June 9   Woodpecker 101
June 12   Red Squirrel 105
June 18   Turtle 108
June 29   Jewelweed 112

SUMMER   117

July 1   Dragonfly 125
July 4   Birch 130
July 7   Bramble 134
July 10   Queen Anne's Lace 139
July 14   Flying Squirrel 141
July 16   Mushroom 144

July 21   Waterlily 147
July 25   Toad 150
July 31   Loon 153
August 3   Whippoorwill 156
August 5   Cattail 158
August 12   Goldenrod 161
August 17   Aster 165
August 23   Caterpillar 167
August 28   Crayfish 172
September 1   Cricket 176
September 8   Fringed Gentian 178
September 26   Sumac 180

AUTUMN   185

October 1   Spider 193
October 4   Sunflower 196
October 18   Owl 199
October 31   White-footed Mouse 202
November 7   Hop Hornbeam Tree 205
November 11   Fox 207
November 15   Salamander 210
November 19   Acorn 214
November 25   Moth 218
December 1   Trout 220
December 6   Skunk 224
December 10   Bayberry 228
December 15   Pine 233
December 27   Goldfinch 236

INDEX   240

FOREWORD

Richard Headstrom seemed to sense that this would be the last of his twenty-five books. He was eighty-two and losing the formidable energy that had produced three other books in the last two years. But he was a determined man. He worked steadily until the day before he entered the hospital for the last time. Even there he muttered, "Got to get back to work." He had been proud of his ability to write publishable books at an age when many men could do little but watch television and attend the funerals of friends.

He had always been a writer. He was only nineteen when a university press issued a little book in which he offered his views on theories of evolution. During the 1920s and '30s he contributed essays on philosophy, literature, and science to magazines. In 1933 he published a history of Russia.

He had begun to realize that his real interest lay in natural science. He started teaching science in private schools, later in Massachusetts public schools. He was a curator in several science museums. He wrote a science column for *The Boston Transcript;* this led to publication of his first "nature" book, *Adventures with a Microscope,* in 1941. He published several other nature books while still a teacher and curator, but more than half of his twenty-five titles were written after his "retirement" in 1964.

It is tempting to conclude that Headstrom's clear and simple style was something he developed during years of communicating difficult scientific ideas to schoolchildren. However, he displayed the same virtues from the beginning: even at nineteen, in his little book on evolution, he handled subtly complex ideas clearly and directly. He was not interested in rhetorical flourishes or beautiful prose, although he occasionally wrote passages with an austere grace of their own. Readers can be grateful that he sought only to give them information as painlessly as possible.

He was blessed with another gift, an enviable one to other writers. When he sat down for his daily stint at the typewriter, he knew not only what he wanted to say but pretty accurately *how* he would say it. Only an unusually orderly mind could have produced such clean copy in first draft. His writing needed little editing by him or anyone else.

Nature for Richard Headstrom was "a world of beauty and splendor, of mystery and the mysterious . . . unbelievable and yet believable." In his last years he could seldom wander in the woods and "poke among the dead leaves for the wild ginger," or "experience a thrill when I come upon a company of Indian pipes rising with ghostly grace from among the brown debris." But he remembered it all and has described it for us, always hoping that his readers would receive from his books what he found in writing them: "an escape, if only temporary, from the tensions and frustrations of modern living."

—Edward Devol

EDITORIAL NOTE: Some of the material in this book has appeared in the author's previous books, sometimes in different form. Mr. Headstrom's writings provided him with a rich lode for publication in many of his volumes, so the present work is in some ways a Richard Headstrom anthology. His death prevented him from editing or organizing this material to his complete satisfaction, but we have endeavored to follow his wishes. In that regard, he indicated dates for some—but not all—of his notebook entries and essays, and we have entered appropriate dates and months to correspond with a year's seasonal cycle and this book's structure as originally envisioned by the author.

Memories from a Naturalist's Notebook is, then, an amalgam—not just a diary of a single year, but a chronicle that combines essays and memories—pages from the author's files, and leaves from his life.

—the editors

W·I·N·T·E·R

January 31 — Snowing. Each season of the year comes with its own sense of beauty and wonder. Everything is outlined in white, simplified. Birds coming and going to feeders, preparing for the forecast of two days of snow, which they seem to "know" and not to hear as we do. A group of house finch arrange themselves on a snowy vine like red-breasted ornaments on a holiday tree. Many colors flashing against snow — blue jay to scarlet red cardinal and his rosy mate — charcoals of the juncos and nuthatches — tweedy brown sparrows and black-and-white checkered woodpeckers — the backyard gang.

It's quiet here and a good time to collect thoughts and soak up the stillness of the woods. Morning is the nicest time of day. A ruffed grouse is drumming while a great horned owl hoots softly in the distance — a wild turkey just gobbled — again. Forest waking up. A woodpecker is hammering down near the swamp. Could be a pileated. A crow is cawing.

Ground pine grows all over the forest in this area — yellow birch and tulip tree (poplar). A little brook ambles through. Purple skunk cabbage heads are arranged among the moss and rocks of the brook.

Wild turkey scratchings in the leaves.

Bark curled, peels in curls.

Tree is shiny yellowish color.

← Yellow birch

The day broke on leaden skies that presaged snowstorm, the kind of sky that Whittier described in "Snowbound." The snowflakes began to fall sometime during the morning. They were light and airy, and the slightest breeze blew them along in whirling dances.

At first, it was a storm much like those we have in early spring that last for a little while and then fade softly away. But this one meant business. The snowflakes continued to come down, and before long it began to appear that a typical New England snowstorm was on its way. Soon the only visible patches of grass to be seen were those around the base of a tree or in a sheltered corner near the house. And then they too disappeared; the world became white. It had become colder, too, and the wind had begun to blow with more intensity.

By midafternoon the stone wall had become all but lost from view and the trees and shrubs across the way but a mere blur. The wind now howled with eerie abandon and blew the flakes into strange domes and towers. All life outdoors seemed to be suspended, waiting for the storm to run its course.

It was still snowing when darkness fell. But during the night the storm passed; as light began to filter through the frosted windows the sun could be seen rising above the horizon in the eastern sky. And when I looked out at the whitened landscape, I was dismayed at the amount of snow that had fallen. I thought that only the tall evergreens in the distance might provide fare for those able to dine at their table; for a time, at least, the fruit-laden shrubs and the withered stalks of weed plants would be no festive board.

Winter, like all seasons, has its disadvantages. But it has its compensations, too. For one thing it is at this time of the year that I really get to know and appreciate the chickadees. When all nature seems to have retired before the icy blasts of the north wind, the chickadee is awing, gay and happy, enlivening the winter scene with his amusing acrobatics and merry chatter. He actually seems to enjoy a snowstorm.

Usually a nuthatch or two may be seen in company with the chickadees; they hunt together all winter for beetles, caterpillars, and the pupae of insects among the cracks and crevices of trees. The nuthatch appears to be a somewhat more industrious bird and pays close attention to the matter at hand, climbing easily straight up or straight down the trunk, or encircling it according to its mood.

In view of the rugged conditions that prevail at this time of the year, it may seem at first rather surprising that there are so many birds with us. But on second thought perhaps this is not so, for birds are normally hardy creatures. On the coldest day I've seen tree sparrows in an open field where the brown stalks of weeds and grasses stand in phalanxes against the sky. Today I watched them for a time and observed them flying with

January 23 – 7 A.M.
Beautiful outside. Snowed all night. Winter chickadees distracting me from my work like children calling another out to play....

I'll be back later — going outside!

dee – dee – dee – look at me —

chickadee working with bill to open sunflower seed.

↑ Grips seed and branch together.

cheerful industry from one brown patch to another, clinging to the dead stalks as they carefully explored them, picking out the seeds. Not only a serious quest for food, it is also a frolic in which their gay notes fall upon the air like the tinkling of sleigh bells. And weedy and bush-grown fields, where the dried and withered stalks trace delicate and intricate shadows on the snow in the bright sunshine, are also hunting grounds for goldfinches and juncoes.

Except for several other species—such as the horned larks that run along the seabeach in merry companies and the snow buntings that habitually seek open fields free from all cover and can be seen along the coast feeding on the seeds of the beach grass—most of our winter birds prefer sheltered places, thickets, and bush-grown roadsides, orchards, cedar and alder swamps, and stands of pine and other coniferous trees. Thus the redpolls (fearless little birds, and usually friendly, but sometimes during the winter season extremely wild) may be observed in an alder swamp; golden-crowned kinglets and brown creepers in oak and maple woods; crossbills and pine grosbeaks in stands of coniferous trees; and cedar waxwings in an orchard. And as I walk through the woods I might hear the tapping of the woodpeckers, or I may find pellets of bone and fur on the snow, evidence that owls have been hunting in the vicinity. If I disturb a grouse in a tangle of bushes, with a thunder of beating pinions it will rise from the ground and take off among the trees, which usually sets a blue jay to screaming and its voice will echo through the woods and fall upon the ears like the sound from a discordant trumpet.

Today, even while I watched the snow, crows streaked across the sky, and probably buffleheads play in the surf along the coast. I think about these birds of the winter landscape, and I know they are out there.

I often go into the fields and woods on a winter's day to escape tribulations of the workaday world. What better panacea can be found than the exhilaration and the glow that comes from walking on the crusty snow and feeling the cold stinging my face. I might pause and watch the goldfinches and tree sparrows feeding in a wind-swept field. I enjoy the inimitable chickadees searching the red fruits of the sumac for hidden insects. I listen to the raucous cry of the blue jay as it breaks the frozen silence.

At this time of the year nature appears to be at a standstill . . . at first glance. To be sure most plant life is dormant and so too are many animals. However, still active are various beetles that live under bark and stones and such winter insects as the springtails, stoneflies, and certain scorpion flies. Even a cricket or grasshopper sometimes may be heard making a lonesome call from the lee of some fence or ledge. Muskrats still forage for the submerged roots and stalks of lilies, cattails, and other water plants, and meadow mice and deer mice continue to feed on the blanched shoots or dried seeds or grasses and to gnaw bark from trees.

January 16 —
Found owl pellet. Broke open to see fur and bones of a rodent — and indigestible.

↓ Fur

Bones

Owl coughs up pellet several hours after eating animal.

Screech owl – one of nature's best little mouse-traps ever built – owl is only about 8 to 10 inches high. This one is grayish brown (can also be reddish brown). Last October a very vocal screech owl in woods near house tuned up many pre-dawn mornings – and some evenings, opening and closing my days with its quavering calls.

Prints in the snow disclose that squirrels, foxes, and mink are up and around and that shrews are very much on the hunt. And beneath the ice-covered ponds one-celled animals, such as *Vorticella* and *Epistylis*, certain worms, and water fleas, are very much alive. But more in evidence are the pine siskens and redpolls that enliven a birch or alder thicket, the juncoes that animate a hemlock grove, the horned larks that in merry companies run along the beach, and the buffleheads that play in the white-crested surf along the coast.

The winter landscape is not without its attractive features, though many see them as bleak and uninviting. The withered grasses, asters, goldenrods, and sunflowers, wreathed in snow or encased in ice, have a graceful glow while the ice-coated catkins of the alders sparkle in the sunshine like jeweled pendants. Then, too, the club mosses give color to the shadowy woodland floor. The green fronds of the Christmas fern brighten the snow-covered woods with winter cheer. The purplish red stems of the red osier add a touch of warmth to the wintry landscape even as the green twigs of the sassafras strike a springlike note in the midst of winter snows.

Undoubtedly the most conspicuous feature of the winter landscape is the trees. Divested of leaves they seem to take on an individuality, more especially when growing in the open and silhouetted against the sky. When I observe the trees at random I have discovered that each species has its own architecture or method of branching. With a little study one may be able to identify any tree at a distance. Thus I've learned to recognize the American elm by its vaselike contour, or the Lombardy poplar by its spirelike form. These are conspicuous examples, but other trees have characteristic outlines by which they, too, may be recognized.

The white oak in the open invariably is two to three times as broad as high. The tulip tree, whose tall, straight trunk rises into the sky like a Corinthian column, has branches comparatively short with upturned tips. How unlike either is the wild black cherry whose contour is quite unconventional, being irregular and rugged with a crooked trunk. Or the yellow willow whose short trunk generally inclines to one side and divides low down into a number of stout, spreading branches that form an irregular broad head. The trunk of the poison sumac also divides low down, forking very near to the ground, the branches, unlike those of the yellow willow, producing a rounded bushy head. Once one has seen an apple tree standing alone, the observer never should have any trouble recognizing it again; it has a short trunk with wide spreading branches that form a characteristic broad, round-topped crown.

In the open and at a distance the sugar maple presents a distinctive appearance, its trunk more or less continuous to the top and with ascend-

Old snow-covered log and fern in the winter woods — a beauty in itself.

ing branches that describe a symmetrical egg-shaped outline when seen against the sky. And the winter hiker can hardly mistake the picturesque flowering dogwood for any other tree since its slender, mostly upright branches and divergent, sinuously curved branchlets that turn upward near their ends are a clue to its identity.

The sycamore is easily recognized by its tapering trunk and by its scraggly branches that form a long egg-shaped figure. So, too, is the mockernut whose trunk is slightly swollen at its base and whose lower branches more or less droop toward the ground. The contorted branches—especially the strongly pendulous lower ones—serve to distinguish the pignut from other trees, as do the zigzag branches of the American hornbeam that are somewhat pendulous at the ends. The zigzag habit of the hornbeam branches even extends to the trunk, which is frequently zigzag above and thus appears to be forked with broad, round crotches.

When silhouetted, the black birch presents an egg-shaped outline and its trunk seems irregularly perpendicular. The trunk of the gray birch generally is inclined to one side, but unlike the yellow willow it has a fringe from top to bottom of short, slender branches that grow upward for a short distance but then bend downward. I have learned that I need only to glance at the tupelo to recognize the uncommonly large number of branches it bears compared to other trees. Although extremely variable in outline, the tupelo can be recognized by its manner of branching. The trunk is erect and usually continuous into the top, with the lower branches well down on the trunk and horizontal or even declined to the ground. The upper branches are horizontal, or somewhat erect, and have many lateral branches and stubby branchlets that form horizontal layers.

The shagbark hickory, so easily identifiable closeup by its shaggy bark, when growing in the forest has a straight trunk that is often free of branches for fifty feet or more. But in the open the shagbark generally forks well down below the middle of the tree. The bitternut also forks well down, but its erect stems form a broad spreading head that is usually widest at the top.

In the swamp white oak the unkempt appearance is due to the numerous tufted, small scraggly, lateral pendant branchlets that develop from the erect upper branches and from the lower ones that are horizontal or even declined to the ground. The sassafras may be distinguished from our other trees by its many stout, horizontal, more or less contorted branches that subdivide to form a dense bushy spray and by a flat-topped or slightly rounded oblong crown it produces. Moreover, as the branches are brittle and easily broken off by wind or ice storms, or by other injuries, this tree often presents a battered appearance. Walking through the winter landscape, I watch for these trees. They seem to signal me, and they tell me who they are.

February 19 —
Two white-tailed deer leap off the road where the high old winter maple stands — not sure which is prettier — the winter deer or the winter maple — but certainly each has a beauty of its own.

JANUARY 3, Bobcat

Today I saw feline tracks in the woods and remembered the first time I saw the tracks of a bobcat. The howl of the wolf, the bark of the fox, and the scream of the bobcat were familiar sounds to the early settlers. The howl of the wolf is gone, but at night people in rural areas still may hear the fox's bark or the bobcat's scream. The bobcat, so called because of its abbreviated tail, is not often seen, like many mammals being most active at night.

A bobcat may venture abroad during the day if restless or hungry, but it rarely takes the chance of exposing itself in broad daylight in settled country. Shy and exceedingly cautious, invariably, on detecting the approach of any invader, it will quietly leave its resting place and silently retreat, giving no sign of its presence, except in winter when its footprints may be seen in the snow.

Indeed, the bobcat is so adept at keeping out of sight that a person might be near one, yet be unaware of its presence. Its tendency to run at the slightest provocation has led to its being described as a timid animal, but if cornered or attacked it becomes a fighter and can take care of itself. Hence, it has few enemies.

True, other predators feint at the bobcat, but the attack is usually perfunctory and quickly abandoned. In farming country, a dog can sometimes be a threat, but a dog really is more of an annoyance because the bobcat is more than a match for it. Actually the bobcat doesn't often find it necessary to make a stand; it usually runs for a short distance and then dives into a rock glen and climbs a tree.

Like many carnivores, the bobcat is not restricted in its diet but feeds on a variety of animals. It hunts by sight more than by scent. Although it feeds avidly on ground-nesting birds, it rarely goes into the trees to hunt. Though a good climber, it is not an arboreal animal and usually takes to a tree only to rest or to find refuge.

Although essentially a silent animal, the bobcat becomes vocal in late February and March, for this is the mating season. Like any cat, the male will howl and squall through a varied repertoire that has an astounding range and volume. So, if I don't actually *see* a bobcat, next month I may hear one.

The bobcat in many ways is like the domestic cat. Like our pet tabby, it frequently limbers up its muscles and sharpens its claws, using a tree trunk for the purpose instead of a piece of furniture. It is fond of catnip and will often roll over and over in the strongly scented herbs, rubbing it into its fur and eating the flowers and leaves.

I was invited to observe and sketch as two bobcats were released today by state biologists in an effort to restore their declining population to former habitats.

← Ear tufts

Beaver pond frozen — can walk on ice out to beaver lodge. Bobcat tracks in the snow. A pileated woodpecker is about. It's cold and there is a snow flurry. A golden sunset glistens across the icy pond. Snowflakes and sun make the air sparkle.

Beaver lodge — beaver safe inside his frozen sanctuary.

Tracks like those of a house cat but larger — four toe pads.

JANUARY 12, Blue Jay

As I watch the blue jays feeding at my seed station just outside my study window (and they are constant visitors), I often think of the many times I used to encounter them on my walks in the snow-covered New England woods. Suddenly I would be startled by one of them taking to wing; it would go flying among the naked branches and at the same time giving voice to that wild frenzied scream with which these birds break the winter silence like the blast of a trumpet.

All living things are part of the environment, but few are so conspicuous as the blue jay, and it would be a sad day indeed were he to disappear forever from the scene. No matter what the season, the blue jay's presence is always welcome. It is a friendly and joyous bird, though perhaps noisy at times and rather prone to shoo away other birds when it arrives at my feeding station. But it is sure to enliven the surroundings wherever it may be with its clownish antics, raising our spirits that flag from the cares and worries with which we all must contend.

There are those that do not like the blue jay because of its propensity to rob the nests of other birds of their eggs and to kill their young; they who would shoot it on sight did they dare. To be sure the jay is guilty of the practice, but it should be remembered that the eggs and nestlings constitute only a fraction of one percent of its diet. As a matter of fact the harm it does is far outweighed by the good, for 20 percent of its diet includes such noxious insects as wood-boring beetles, grasshoppers, various caterpillars, and scale insects. But who are we to indict the blue jay because of habits it inherited from some remote ancestor; indeed, who are we to question the designs of nature. Moreover, there are other birds that prey on their kind more extensively than the blue jay does.

There are some that say the blue jay is a handsome bird; there are others that take a contrary view. Doubtless there are birds with a more brilliant plumage or with colors that more quickly attract the eye. But at least the blue jay puts its colors to advantage. From a little concealment I have watched a blue jay wing its way among the leafless trees, a conspicuous and lovely object, and then land on a distant branch and disappear from view, merely by alighting in such a way that its colors blend with the sky's.

At a certain time of the year the blue jay is not much in evidence, for it is then occupied with domestic chores. But when nesting duties have been completed and it is free to revel in the plenty that nature has provided, it will join with other jays; then the autumn woods will resound with their

Ever-confident bluejay — sure of himself and his place at the bird feeder — the "town crier" of the woodlands!

jay
jay
jay

Blue jays are beautiful now. Bright blue accent color against the white snow, soft browns and grays of a winter day. So as not to go unnoticed, they make sure I know they're here with robust calls as they cover the countryside.

cries as they fly among the treetops, a boisterous, rollicking crew screaming at the top of their voices as if in mortal terror, but apparently for no other reason than to exercise their vocal chords. Yet their din is not without value: As the hunting season opens it serves as a warning to the four-footed creatures to scurry for cover. I enjoy blue jays!

JANUARY 19, Junco

Today I saw my first junco, the first of this winter. There is a layer of snow on the ground, not deep enough to make walking arduous but deep enough to take clear, well-formed prints and tracks. The sun shone brightly in a rather cloudless sky, and there was little if any wind, merely a mild breeze but sufficiently strong to set the leafless twigs of the trees into performing intricate dance steps in the air. It was the kind of day to entice one outdoors and it reminded me of my first junco seen many winters ago.

One day after lunch a friend of mine and I set out for a walk through the woods that lay about half a mile from where we lived. We knew the woods well, having visited it innumerable times during the warmer parts of the year, but this was our first visit during that winter season. We walked about somewhat aimlessly, exploring the woods in the manner that boys are apt to do (I was in my teens at the time) and had not been in the woods too long when we heard a series of twitterings that appeared to come from a hemlock grove just a short distance ahead. We made our way toward it and soon came upon a flock of some dozen or so gray and white little birds fluttering about on the snow and all twittering together. It was a memorable scene, as I had never seen juncoes before, one which I have never forgotten; the sombre dress of the birds provided a pleasing contrast to their surroundings.

Originally the junco was known as the snowbird and still is to some degree. I rather prefer "snowbird" as I think it has more charm and appeal, especially to children. And the poet I can see writing about the snowbird—but about the "junco"? But some time ago the scientists decreed that the bird should be called the junco, a decision never satisfactorily explained as the word means *rush*, an odd name to give a bird that habitually occupies the woodlands and thickets.

The junco we know so well in the Northeast is the species called the dark-eyed junco, a name quite descriptive of its appearance. (The old name was slate-colored junco, and there are a number of species and subspecies.) Its scientific name is *hyemalis*, more in keeping with the bird's habitats for it means "wintry" in Latin. The Latin in turn comes from the Greek *cheimon*, which is related to the Sanskrit *hima* or "snow."

The junco is a true winter bird, remaining in its northern breeding range well into fall and then going south only when its food supply begins to dwindle. Presumably the name snowbird was earned originally because its arrival in its southern range supposedly foretold the coming of winter and the appearance of snow.

January 1 —
Winter storm — snowing hard —
junco perched on the
pine bough near the
feeder. It's wearing
a bird band.
Snowflakes on
back of gray bird
are very soft looking.
Downy feathers fluffed
out to contain body heat.

Numbered bird band on junco's leg.

Snow bird!

In Massachusetts the junco usually appeared in my garden sometime during October, several weeks ahead of the first snowfall. I would see it intermittently throughout the winter, more frequently if the winter were a severe one, appearing at my feeding stations for the bounty I would provide for all the avian visitors and guests. Someone once described the junco as "leaden skies above, snow below," and how apt the expression is when the bird is seen on a gray winter's day when the skies promise a fall of snow. The coloring of the junco—slate gray above and white below—stands the bird in good stead as an effective protective coloration. Moreover, its color pattern is an excellent example of countershading, that is, the bird is darkest above, where it receives the most light, and lightest below, where it receives the most shadow. This kind of coloration tends to destroy the apparent solidity of the bird and make it appear flat, so that it blends into the background and becomes part of it. The junco also exhibits what is known as deflective coloration, its flashing white outer tail feathers being used to divert the aim of a pursuing predator from a more vital part of the bird's body.

The juncoes have the habit of assembling in the fall in small flocks and staying together in close association until spring. At this time they may often be seen in neglected, brush-covered fields and weedy gardens. As the cold weather sets in and the snow begins to fly, however, they seek the vicinity of farmyards and houses where they are generally not disappointed in finding an ample food supply. During the winter they remain within a narrowly circumscribed range and rarely move farther than to a neighboring weed patch for a change of diet or to a nearby grove of evergreens, there to roost and find shelter from the elements.

With the return of warmer weather in the spring, the juncoes take leave of their human benefactors and seek the fields and woodland borders. Here they are joined by others that have spent the winter in more southern climes, and soon they set out for their breeding grounds in the northern coniferous country of New England and Canada. (Though some may nest in the highlands of Pennsylvania, New York, and western Massachusetts.)

March 2 —
Juncos pursuing each other all over the yard — flying fast, dodging and weaving among obstacles — chasing here — catching perhaps farther north.

Courtship and nesting preliminaries.

JANUARY 26, Insect

The protectively varnished egg bands of the tent caterpillar are conspicuous on the twigs of wild cherries, and equally conspicuous on the bark of elms and maples are the egg masses of the white-marked tussock moth, attached to the loose cocoons of the wingless females. The light buff oval masses of the gypsy moth may be found on the trunks of trees, on fences, in the crevices of rocks, on piles of wood, and in similar places; and the curious egg sacs of the bagworm are to be seen hanging starkly from the twigs of trees.

The naturalist with a discerning eye may well find the larvae of the pistol-case bearer hibernating in pistol-shaped cases attached to apple twigs; the larvae of the cattail moth wintering in frayed cattail heads; half-grown larvae of the viceroy butterfly in silken cases, suspended from the twigs of poplar and sassafras; the green or ashen gray chrysalides of the cabbage butterfly fastened to fences and buildings by tufts of silk; and the pupae of the cecropia moth hidden away in the large silken cases noticeably suspended from the twigs of various trees and once called by children the "cradle-cocoon."

Insects, however, are not entirely dormant during the winter. Various stone flies complete their nymphal lives in ice-rimmed streams, appearing in the wintry air as adults and mating on the banks. Springtails often mass in dark patches on the quiet waters of still unfrozen ponds. The larvae of caddis flies may be seen crawling over the bottom of streams or clinging to the stalks of submerged water plants. The nymphs of various mayflies are abundant in swift rivulets and spring-fed brooks. And on warm sunny days diving beetles often rise to the surface of ponds and streams.

Snowflies may also be seen walking over the snow, bluebottle and greenbottle flies may be observed emerging from their retreats in the corners of attics and the crevices of outbuildings, and gnats fly forth in small swarms or by the thousands. Mourning-cloak butterflies are also to be observed flitting about in a sunny glade.

The winter hiker may well wonder what the little black specks are that spring away on either side of one's feet as you walk over the snow on a bright warm winter day, or that hop about on the snow on the sunny side of a tree trunk like so many miniature jumping jacks. Sometimes there are so many of them that the snow appears to be sprinkled with numberless grains of pepper.

These little animated black specks are commonly called snowfleas, a most descriptive term. Actually they are a type of springtail of which there

Took a walk and found snowfleas by a tree. Millions of them!

Snowfleas on the snow — little jumping specks.

are some 2000 species. Now if you set about catching a few of these snowfleas, as I did when I first saw them, and look at them closely with a magnifying glass or hand lens, you will find that they are the most grotesque-looking animals. If you know something about animal anatomy you will observe that they have three distinct body regions—namely a head, thorax, and abdomen—and that they must therefore be insects. And perhaps you may wonder what happened to their wings, as all insects appear to have them. But springtails never did have wings and probably never will. It was once thought that springtails are degenerate descendants of winged creatures, but the present view is that they are primitive insects—in other words that they appeared on the earth before insects acquired wings. Indeed, some authorities even claim that they are not insects at all but a group of *Arthropods* (a phylum of invertebrate animals with segmented legs) below the level of the true insects and cite certain peculiarities in their embryonic development and adult morphology to substantiate their view. But we know them as insects, as most entomologists consider them to be.

The jumping or leaping ability of the springtail is due to a springlike structure on the lower surface of the abdomen. It consists of a pair of appendages united at the base but separated at the other ends so as to form a two-pronged fork. This forklike structure (called the *furcula*) projects forward and is caught in a toothed structure (called the *tenaculum*) much like the spring of a mousetrap. When the springtail wishes to jump, it activates the tenaculum so that it releases the furcula, which then springs back and catapults the insect into the air. You can easily see the jumping mechanism of the springtail with your hand lens. How high can a springtail jump? About eight inches, which compares favorably with the flea.

The springtails made their appearance on the earth some millions of years ago. As they are still on the earth, they must be adaptable creatures. Hence it is not surprising to find that they are widely distributed, from the Arctic to the Antarctic, some species being year-round residents of the Antarctic continent.

It's January, but insects are still present everywhere as eggs, larvae or nymphs, pupae, and hibernating adults. They are not, however, conspicuously present as they will be in the warmer months when they may be seen flying, crawling, and jumping wherever we look. Nor is this the time of the year when we normally expect them to mate. But some do, including certain species of stoneflies, of which there are some 1500.

To an entomologist a stonefly is not a true fly—which has but a single pair of wings (or at least most do)—for the stonefly has two pairs. There are other differences, too. Stoneflies have only three stages in their life history: egg, nymph or naiad, and adult; the true flies have four: egg, larva, pupa, and adult.

Adult stoneflies are dull colored, with usually long wings that are held folded back lengthwise over the body when at rest, making them appear elongated, with their long antennae pointing forward and their two fairly long abdominal appendages (*cerci*) directed backward.

Adult stoneflies for the most part prefer shade, normally remaining in seclusion in shrubbery and vegetation (though some species may be seen in bright sunlight on the winter snow), and they are not as a rule found far from the water from which they emerged. The nymphs are aquatic in habit, and according to the species occur in larger or smaller streams, in swift or moderate currents, or on rocky stream beds, where algae on which to feed is plentiful as well as other plants. Some even feed on aquatic insects.

Stoneflies spend the greater part of their lives in water, the nymphs transforming into adults in a distinct seasonal succession, from late fall to late summer. As one writer has put it, "The fact that about one-third of the species of the order *Plecoptera* (stoneflies) *Illinois* emerge as adults, mate,

Snow and ice on the ground. Across the brook and through the woods a phoebe is tail wagging on a branch. Then it swoops down on the snow after something. Is Phoebe swooping after snowfleas, perhaps? Or some other early insect?

Stoneflies in the yard next to brook — on laundry basket and me. On the stones near the water, I caught one easily and sketched it. Fitting name!

Stoneflies crawl over stones. *Gray color.*

feed, and carry on all seasonal activities for the perpetuation of the species in the coldest months of the year is indeed unique among the major insect orders. . . ."[1]

The nymphs, generally sluggish animals, rest in debris or algae or cling to the undersides of rocks in swift water; they are rarely found in poorly oxygenated or polluted streams. Most of them have tracheal gills that usually occur on the ventral surface of the thorax. They live from one to three years and crawl out of the water when ready to transform.

Unlike the species that mature in summer, those that reach adulthood in winter take food freely then, foraging in the daytime on the green and blue-green algae found on tree trunks. They mate while creeping or resting and never while in flight. They are often quite numerous and may easily be collected at their feeding places. After mating, the females of some species crawl to the edge of the stream and lay their eggs in the water; others fly low over the water and drop their eggs into it, or even alight on the surface.

The love life of these creatures shows there's more to January than meets the eye.

[1]Frison, T. H. (1935). Stoneflies or Plecoptera of Illinois. *Ill. Nat. Hist. Survey Bull.* 20 (4).

FEBRUARY 5, Shrew

When February arrives on the calendar and leaden skies promise still more snow, my thoughts always turn to those birds and mammals that do not retreat before falling temperatures and chilling winds but remain with us throughout winter.

These animals have little fear of the rigors of winter. For many it is a challenge that tests their courage and ingenuity; they match wits against their enemies and try to circumvent the conditions that deprive them of food by covering the ground with a blanket of snow and encasing trees and shrubs in icy pendants.

Most amazing to me is how the shrew gets through this period. One would expect this tiny animal to hibernate, but instead it is up and around during all hours and in all sorts of weather. Because of its small size, quick movements, and its habit of working under cover, I seldom actually see it. Occasionally I have come upon it poking its delicate snout into crevices in the bark on the lower part of a treetrunk or ferreting about in leaf mold or among decaying pieces of wood for its accustomed prey. More commonly I have found its elfinlike tracks in the snow, sometimes in my own back yard.

Because of a very rapid rate of digestion, the shrew requires an enormous amount of food and literally eats all the time, and deprived of food for even several hours it will starve to death. Its food consists of insects, snails, small annelids, and other such animals as it can capture. It seems incredible that it can find such fare in sufficient amounts during the winter to sustain life, generating enough body heat to offset low temperatures.

But apparently there are enough dormant insects available to supply its needs. True, it can live on a plant menu for many days, but plants are eaten sparingly and only if its preferred diet is unobtainable.

People often mistake a shrew for a mouse or mole. Superficially it resembles both of these animals, but it may easily be distinguished from the mole by its smaller size and mouselike feet, and from the mouse by its pointed nose, small eyes, and finer fur.

The common shrew is one of the smallest of mammals. It measures barely four inches in length and weighs four to five grams. Yet in spite of its diminutive size it is a highly predatory, courageous, and pugnacious little animal that will not hesitate to attack creatures several times its own weight, such as mice, whenever these rodents are encountered.

I have never ceased to marvel how the shrew has been able to hold its own against a host of natural enemies and varying climatic conditions, because it ranges as far north as the Arctic Circle. How many shrews fall

Bear Swamp

Sitting in the woods, I keep hearing rustling noises but can't find the source. There he is — a shrew, picking among leaves and moss to find a meal and satisify his ever-constant appetite. If he's not quiet, he's going to satisify the appetite of an owl that I know lives here too!

victim to the owls, hawks, shrikes, herons, foxes, and weasels that prey upon them with impunity can be seen by the large number of their bones that are contained in owl pellets alone.

Yet the shrew is widely distributed and is abundant in many places. I suspect one reason for its survival is that it is able to make its home wherever there is food and shelter, being as much at home in the dark moss-carpeted forests of the north as in the deciduous woods and the grassy fields and meadows farther south.

Bear Swamp — light covering of snow on the ground — sitting in woods, I can hear a distant siren — even this far away — can hear it plainly. A barred owl seems to be responding to the fire siren's wail with calls of its own. Owl pellets in this area — I wonder if the little shrew is in one of these pellets!

← Brown eyes

A pair of barred owls heard here.

FEBRUARY 10, Kinglet

Whenever I have seen one of the kinglets it has always been a memorable occasion, for we seldom get the chance to see one of these diminutive birds—at least close enough to identify it. There are two species, the golden-crowned and the ruby-crowned. I often see the golden-crowned in small flocks in the evergreens, where they remain for the most part hidden by the greenery but appear now and then like a flicker of green and gold on the tips of the branches, and I can identify them by their nervous habit of flipping up their wingtips.

The kinglet is so named because of the colored patch on top of the head that suggests a crown. In the ruby-crowned the patch is scarlet, in the male golden-crowned orange and in the female yellow. In the golden-crowned the colored patch may easily be seen if the bird's head is in full view, although in the thick foliage of the conifers the bird may not be easily seen; among deciduous trees, however, it is quite conspicuous. It is quite the contrary for the ruby-crowned, however, whose colored patch is partly or entirely concealed by feathers and is evident only when the bird becomes excited, as when the male is courting the female.

These dainty little feathered creatures that John Burroughs so aptly called "Hop-o-My-Thumbs" are the smallest of our birds, with the exception of the hummingbird. There is but slight difference in their size and little in their general coloration except for the distinctive marks as indicated by their name. Their habits are also similar.

Neither of the kinglets is a pugnacious or quarrelsome bird, although at times they may appear to be as when the males are vying for the same female. They are both essentially peaceable birds, and as a rule the ruby-crowned is so absorbed in whatever business engages him at the time that we can approach within a few feet of him.

Golden-crowned kinglets are not uncommon in winter and in spite of their fragile appearance seem to enjoy the bitterest and stormiest winter weather; they always seem cheerful and industrious at such times, much like the chickadees in whose company they are often to be found. Apparently it is not so much a matter of temperature as of food. Given plenty of the latter, they appear to have no difficulty in surviving.

The songs of the two kinglets differ greatly. That of the golden-crowned begins with a series of shrill, high-pitched, somewhat quavering notes and ends in a rather explosive chickadeelike chatter. That of the ruby-crowned is more elaborate and musical and, for so small a bird, is usually loud and clear with a remarkable sweetness and brilliance of tone. It begins with several high notes, then several low notes, and ends in a repetitious chant.

Hovering for an instant.

← yellow

Golden-crowned kinglet hovers before alighting on branch — not unlike hummingbird. High delicate note accompanies the bird.

April 27 —
Saw ruby-crowned kinglet in the woods just behind barn. Could clearly see crown of red with field glasses. Saw him three different times among red cedars and white pine. He passes through so quickly on migration that he's easy to miss. Rue anemone and wood anemone flowering — trailing arbutus too. Mayapple leaves up and open. Columbine growing out of the top of a limestone rock in only a few grains of soil.

Ruby red crown.

Blue cedar berries.

FEBRUARY 21, Mourning Cloak Butterfly

The snow may be high on the ground, the temperature may be subzero, and the wind may howl over the landscape. Hardly the time to think of butterflies, and yet within a few days they may be seen flitting about in some sunny spot in the still leafless woods. For the weather may change, and a midwinter thaw set in that beckons forth the mourning cloak butterfly. This is the large purplish-brown butterfly with the light-bordered wings we so often see in the summer flitting about lazily in the sunshine. But late winter is a time of contrasts, when there are days with spring in the air—days when the mercury climbs high and howling winds give way to zephyrs; when a benign sun warms the earth and melting snows cascade along rock-ribbed gullies—so we should not be too surprised at what we may see. Any day now, I know I'll see a mourning cloak.

The mourning cloak butterfly hibernates as an adult in some convenient shelter, but on warm days during the winter it often emerges and flies about from tree to tree. It stays out only during the warmer hours of the day; as the temperature begins to drop it returns to its winter quarters, where it remains until the sun again warms it into activity. Once it has left its winter quarters for good it seeks the sap of maple trees where squirrels have gnawed the bark and also visits the stumps of newly cut trees for the exuding sap. And when the willow catkins dance upon the south wind we may find it sipping the nectar secreted by the blossoms, and later when the mayflower blooms we may come across it hovering about the fragrant flowers for a similar purpose.

When the aphids become sufficiently abundant so that their "honey dew" may be found on infested shrubs, the butterfly frequently sips the sweet liquid from the surface of the leaves, and from the time the early apples begin to ripen it is a frequent visitor to the orchard, sipping the juice from the fallen and decaying fruit.

About the time of maple sap running — I see the mourning cloak butterfly just out of hibernation, gathering its first meal — a sip of sap from broken ends of branches or holes in the trunk.

Mourning cloak sitting on dead grass stalks on the ground. Beautiful contrast of colors in the bright sun.

MARCH 5, Hepatica

For years botanists and naturalists have been undecided as to which of the two plants, the hepatica and the skunk cabbage, is the first to flower in the spring. The question may never be resolved, and but these two wildflowers are among the first to blossom, at least in the north.

It was a long time ago that I found my first hepatica, blossoming beneath a blanket of snow, and it was a never-forgotten experience. One must be insensitive, indeed, to ignore the irresistible charm of this lovely and seemingly delicate flower that adds a note of cheerfulness to the still-bleak woods and thrills a strolling wanderer with its unexpected beauty.

Some books say that the hepatica begins to flower in February, others in March, and still others in April, but all agree that it continues to blossom until May. The flowers vary in color—blue, lavender, purple, lilac, pink, or white—and in fragrance as well. Sometimes it is the purple flowers that are sweet-scented, sometimes the white, sometimes the pink. I can discover those that are fragrant only by trying them. The odor, which at no time is very strong, reminds me of violets.

Unless one has found the hepatica before and knows where to look, it will likely be found only by chance, beneath the decaying leaves of the woodland floor, in some hidden nook, or beneath the lingering snows that have escaped the warm rays of the spring sun. If the early spring backpacker happens to have a hand lens or magnifying glass in pocket or pack, it's rewarding to examine the flowers at close range. What seem to be petals are instead colored sepals, leaflike structures that enclose and protect the other floral organs within the bud before they are fully developed. Three small, sessile leaves form an involucre directly beneath the flower. They simulate a calyx and might easily be mistaken for one.

The leaves are three-lobed—hence the specific name of *triloba*—olive-green, somewhat leathery, and last throughout the winter; they extend from the root and spread on the ground. Those of the preceding year are rusty and remain so until some time after the blossoms have appeared, when the fresh young leaves begin to uncurl. These newer leaves, together with the leaf stems and flower stems, are covered with fuzzy hair, as if nature designed a fur coat to protect this delicate-seeming plant from the icy blasts of departing winter and the chilly nights of the newborn spring.

The generic name *Hepatica*, which is also the common name, is from the Greek for liver and was given to the plant because its leaves have a fancied resemblance to that organ. Hence, the plant is also popularly known as the liverwort or liverleaf. Because of this supposed resemblance, and because it was believed in early times that nature indicated in some

March 17 — Amazing sight to see violet-colored hepatica flowers surrounded by snow! The flowers pushed up to the sun at the base of a tree — like tiny jewels. I come here when I want to see early wildflowers — on the sunny side of my brook.

such fashion the uses to which her plant creations might be applied, the hepatica or liverwort was employed as a specific for all kinds of ailments that affected the liver.

It is doubtful if insects are necessary to the ferilization of the hepatica as these flowers can fertilize themselves, but pollen-feeding flies and female hive bees do visit the blossoms. Early butterflies may also be seen about the flowers, but whether they obtain any nectar appears to be a moot question.

March 21 —

Beautiful hepatica — pink, purple, and violet colors pushing up through the wood's floor. It doesn't put forth new leaves until after the flowers bloom. Such a welcome, delicate sight for March.

about life size.
← stems have tiny hairs.

Old leaves
← green and maroon colored — also called liver leaf.

MARCH 13, Grackle

I saw the grackles for the first time on an early spring day like today. They were presumably newly returned from the south and had taken temporary possession of an old field. Through this field they walked with their heads held nearly level and with all the dignity they could muster, their colors iridescent in the bright spring sun.

    I watched them for a while noting every movement as they walked about, their tails swinging slightly from side to side. But suddenly, apparently frightened, they rose as one and flew to the top of a still leafless tree. There they settled on the bare branches and gave voice to what they most likely considered to be a song, but to me it was anything but musical. Yet musical or not, it is one of nature's sounds worth hearing.

    The grackle, or "crow blackbird" as it was once known, is essentially a bird of the marsh and waterside of the forested regions of the country, but as grackles became gradually settled they found a new food supply in the form of the corn crop. They not only multiplied exceedingly but gradually became birds of more open country and farmlands, and at the same time learned to come into cities and villages and to nest in trees in parks and cemeteries. The grackle, a bird that ranks high in intelligence, is altogether a most interesting bird. It often appears on our lawn or garden and we always welcome it (though it has one fault, that of preying on eggs and young birds, and occasionally on adults as well). The grackle is fond of water and often bathes in it and sometimes catches small fish. It is more or less an omnivorus bird, very fond of insects, and in autumn when grain, fruits, nuts, and seeds become plentiful it invariably turns to such fare. But it has the bad habit of pecking at apples and pears and leaving the half-eaten fruit to rot on the ground.

May 15 —
A grackle is feeding on beaver dam, picking about sticks and leaves. It disturbed a water snake that crawled out. Grackle jumped back in surprise. When feeding in mud, grackle appears to put closed bill in mud, then opens it to spread leaves and the mud, probing for a meal.

MARCH 16, Spring Azure Butterfly

Ever since I can remember, the bluebird has been regarded as the first harbinger of spring in New England, and when we first catch a flash of cerulean color among the naked branches of a roadside maple or an apple tree in the orchard we know that winter is on the brink of leaving us. But there are other harbingers, to be sure, such as the hepatica that we often find blossoming beneath the snow and the skunk cabbage in the swamp. Another is the spring azure butterfly, which, having recently emerged from an overwintering pupa, can often be seen flitting about like a "violet afloat"—as Scudder so happily put it—in the still bleak woods patched with snow here and there, or fluttering about the dogwood blossoms and the early spring flowers.

The spring azure is one of the first of our native species of butterflies to appear in the spring, and we may well wonder why nature selected this dainty little creature to be its herald. It would somehow seem more fitting if some larger and more robust butterfly were to signal the end of the long period of cold and inactivity and the awakening of life throughout the nature world.

Of a delicate blue color and measuring scarcely an inch across its outstretched wings, the spring azure is a creature of many fashions. For not only do we find one form of this butterfly in one locality and a different one in another, but even seasonally it differs to a marked degree. Thus we have in the vicinity of Boston an early spring form that is small with large black markings on the undersurface of the wings, a later variety that is larger with small black spots, and finally in summer a third form that is still larger and with considerably fainter spots. The spring azure exhibits polymorphism to an extent not exhibited by any other known species, there being in the United States alone thirteen or more named forms, and in the Old World many other forms have been described.

The spring azure may be found in brushy areas, along the edges of woods, but most typically it is sighted in open, deciduous woodlands. Watch it sometime; you will observe that it has a rather slow, fluttering flight and is often to be seen high among the buds and leaves of trees.

The females lay their eggs among the flower buds, where they are often tucked away out of sight, and on the leaves of such food plants as the flowering dogwood, meadowsweet, New Jersey tea, maple-leaved viburnum, blueberry, black snakeroot, and various species of sumacs on which the larvae feed. The caterpillars are sluglike, whitish, and rose-tinted, with a faint dusky stripe along the back and very faint, oblong, greenish stripes along the sides. The head is dark chestnut and the body has short, white hairs. The upper surface of the chrysalis, which is usually attached to the food plant, is a light brownish-yellow with a very faint yellow-brown dorsal line; the lower surface is yellowish, sparsely and faintly sprinkled with dark-brown dots arranged in longitudinal rows.

The caterpillars are no less interesting than the adults with their many forms. If you look at one with a hand lens or magnifying glass you will find on the back of the seventh and eighth abdominal segments a small opening, the external opening of an eversible sac that secretes a sweet liquid—the sac or gland—called an *osmeterium*. Now it so happens that the ants are fond of this liquid and by stroking the caterpillars with their antennae are able to induce the latter to excrete it. Years ago the American naturalist Edwards pointed out that in return for this largess, the ants chase away parasitic flies that seek to lay their eggs in the caterpillars. So what may seem at first to be a one-sided relationship between the ants and the caterpillars is actually one of mutual benefit.

March 15 —
Not yet the first day of spring (March 20) but very much a spring day — bluebird pair seen — kids talking of trout fishing and baseball — the spirits of folks are lighter and full of sunshine — talk of vegatable gardens and early peas. Many signs of spring are everywhere.

Pair of bluebirds in apple tree — and a young man's (bird's) fancy turns to love — in the spring!

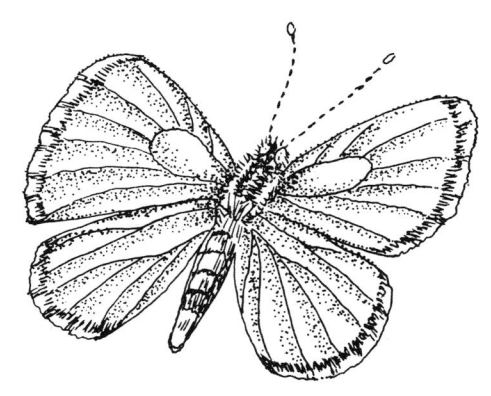

April 17 —
In the forest today I saw the early blue butterfly (azure) floating about. Small, only about an inch long, and a beautiful lavender blue — I've seen them in March too — just when a little color is needed after a long gray and white winter.

MARCH 22, Bumblebee

Spring is always the time of great expectations and many surprises. Thus, I never know when I might catch a glimpse of the first bluebird, robin, or phoebe, whose arrival is so eagerly awaited, or when I shall find the first spring wildflower. Perhaps it will be the hepatica hidden among the decaying leaves of the woodland floor, or the delicate anemone of fragile beauty, trembling in the spring breezes as they weave gently in and out among the trees, or the common violet "half hidden from the eye, fair as a star, when only one is shining in the sky."

Although I may be thrilled by a glimpse of some first arrival from the southland or by the discovery of some early blossom, like many people, I sometimes take the appearance of the first bumblebee as a matter of course. Yet, the sight of a bumblebee flying low over a field or meadow in early spring is always a source of much delight. I suspect the bumblebees have always fascinated me partly because they seem to prove an exception to the rule of "business before pleasure."

Few of us know that these early bees are the queens upon whom falls the duty of founding new colonies and thus perpetuating the species. They are the only survivors of last year's colonies, and how they manage to get through the winter is something we do not know. But they take their destiny lightly and, before they settle down to more serious matters, they fly about and scout for a nest site. They sip the nectar of early flowers and fill the baskets on their hind legs with pollen grains. They have had nothing to eat for eight or nine months, and no one can work well on an empty stomach.

At last, having had their fill of food and feeling fit to work, they begin to look for a suitable place in which to build their nest. They search carefully and diligently for some abandoned, usually underground, nest of a field mouse or chipmunk, although sometimes they will use an empty bird's nest. Upon finding one to her taste, the queen mixes the pollen and nectar that she has gathered into a loaf about the size of a bean, which she places on the floor of the nest. On this mass of "beebread" she lays a few tiny eggs and covers them with wax she exudes from between her abdominal segments. Then she proceeds to make a thimblelike honey pot that she fills with honey, to serve as food while she broods over her eggs until they hatch.

Upon hatching, the young larvae feed upon the "beebread" under the waxen coverlet, which the queen pierces from time to time so that the larvae may have access to the food. As they feed, the larvae burrow deeper and deeper into the "beebread," each one making a cave for itself. When

April 19 —
Spring beauty growing in groups near trees — color varies from deep pink to almost white — four to ten inches or so high — smell of cow manure strong here — cows graze these woods and fields. A bumblebee just visited some of these wildflowers. Also blooming here are trout lilies, violets, wild oats in bud (bellwort), and I just saw a meadowlark.

full grown, in about a week or so, each larva spins for itself a thin, papery but tough cocoon and pupates. Meanwhile the queen broods on the cocoons and sips from her honey pot.

About ten days or two weeks later, the larvae emerge as adult bumblebees. They are smaller than the queen and are known as the "workers"; upon them now fall the tasks of gathering nectar and pollen and adding them to the mass of "beebread" and of helping to rear other workers. The queen from now on devotes her entire energies to laying eggs. Later the workers strengthen the silken pupa cradles with wax and convert them into cells for storing honey.

The first generation of workers is soon followed by others, and the colony gradually increases in size until the climax is reached in late summer, when young queens and males are finally produced. Then, as summer wanes, the workers begin to die off, soon followed by the males after they have mated with the queens. The mother queen, having fulfilled her destiny, also dies, leaving only the young queens. They search for some cozy retreat in which to spend the winter, usually in the ground from two inches to a foot beneath the surface. These are the bumblebees I will see the following spring, some fine day in March.

April 12 —
Loud buzzing coming from a bumblebee — first one I've seen this year. It flew past me in woods near the ground. Very large, fuzzy bee.

MARCH 28, Ladybug

As I write these lines my thoughts go back some seventy years, to a day in March when the temperature outdoors rose to an unseasonable degree, as it sometimes did, and warmed into life some ladybird beetles—or ladybugs, as we called them; they had wintered in our house presumably in some sheltered place like the attic. My mother did not tolerate insects in the house, but she made an exception in the case of the ladybugs because, she said, they brought luck and money whenever they appeared in the house. I don't believe she had much faith in the superstition, but it is an age-old belief that goes back to the Middle Ages, when the beetles were dedicated to the Virgin Mary and became known as the "beetles of the Blessed Virgin."

I had seen the beetles before and had given them little thought, but this time for some inexplicable reason I looked at them a little more closely and became fascinated by their bright colors and varied designs. On the spur of the moment I decided to collect as many different kinds as I could find. It was the beginning of my first insect collection, to be followed by many others through the ensuing years.

Some time later a friend of the family, one knowledgeable about insects, dropped in for a visit. Upon seeing my collection of beetles, he suggested that instead of killing them I should let them live since they performed a valuable service in destroying vast quantities of aphids and scale insects. He then told me the story of the vedalia beetle.

Toward the close of the last century the citrus growers of California were suddenly threatened with the loss of their crops by the ravages of the cottony-cushion scale, which somehow had managed to get into our country from abroad. Our native species of ladybugs were not interested in the newcomer, various insecticidal sprays proved ineffective, and other methods of control were equally unsuccessful. So the problem became one of finding some insect that would prey on the pest, and thus keep it under control. After considerable searching such an insect was discovered in the form of an Australia ladybug generally known as the vedalia beetle. It was brought to California, though not without some trouble, and did the job so well that the beetle itself almost died out for a lack of food; as a matter of fact it became necessary for the state of California to undertake the artificial propagation of the vedalia beetle to insure a continuous supply. Millions of these beetles are now reared and liberated each year in various orchards in an effort to keep the cottony-scale insect under control. I have related the story of the vedalia beetle to my classes and in my lectures whenever feasible through the years: The introduction of the beetle to prey on the scale insects was the first example of what is now known as biological control, that is, the control of an insect pest by means of another insect instead of by insecticides or by crop rotation.

And perhaps the ladybug I found in my study today will bring me "luck and money."

March 29 —
Windows open today — letting spring come in — a ladybug beetle in the house, up and about, sitting on the window sill. Ladybug, ladybug — find them wintering with me — fly away home — they always surprise me as being out of season. Picked her up and put her in another protected corner of the house to await the coming of spring.

April 28 —
Changed the clock last night and gained an hour of daylight — or so it seems. Walking today in the woods enjoying wildflowers in bloom. Rue anemone and violets. Wild columbine bouncing in the sunlight attracting birds and butterflies. I usually see columbines growing in the rocks where soil collects or on the hillsides.

SPRING

May 13 —

Apple blossoms out — pair of screech owls raising owlets in one of the trees in our orchard. May seems to be the month in motion — birds, trees, and flowers. As in a time-exposure photograph, I can almost see May open her apple blossoms, her sugar maples, her birches and lilacs — redecorating the nurseries for the young of the year.

On the calendar, Washington's birthday is a sort of turning point in the nature world. To be sure it is still a winter holiday, but with its arrival we know there are only a few more days until March, a capricious month, promising much and frequently fooling us all. With March is sounded the death knell of winter, and spring is on its way. And many of us are early afield to seek the skunk cabbage or to search more painstakingly for the hepatica, the advance guard of the parade of flowers.

Whether skunk cabbage or hepatica blossoms first is a moot question that will never be settled to everyone's satisfaction. Neither will the debate as to whether the American elm or the silver maple is the first to bring forth its blossoms. It is of no great moment; more important is that all herald spring.

As I write I wonder how many are aware of trees when they are in flower, except when a magnolia is in bloom or a dogwood or apple tree may be seen in someone's yard, or when the flowers of the shadbush may be observed gleaming like white stars in the wildwood.

It is the law of the woods that forest trees shall bring forth blossoms before leaves. The poplars and aspens, the American elm, and silver and red maples blossom in early spring; the birches, oaks, and hickories somewhat later. The American elm, which can trace its lineage to the Miocene, is one of the first of our trees to blossom. Before April is well under way the buds shake off their brown scales and invest the tree in a coppery mist. I looked closely at an elm twig and found eight to twenty tiny flowers in umbellike clusters. Through a hand lens they become most attractive with their bell-shaped reddish-green calyx cups, bright-red anthers, and pale-green pistils.

While it is not essential to the appreciation of tree blossoms, the fact that among some species trees may be either female or male helps in understanding the differences that may appear in the flowers of two different trees of the same species. Species in which all the flowers of an individual tree are either male or female are called dioecious. Botanists normally refer to the female flowers as pistillate or fertile and to the male flowers as staminate or sterile. In conventional terms, the tree bearing male flowers is not sterile; the term "sterile" in this sense means only that the individual tree does not bear fruit.

Sometimes even before the elm has blossomed, depending on ecological factors, the silver maple opens its greenish-yellow flowers and soon the red maple follows. Some red maples appear very red when in blossom while others appear yellowish. The difference is due to the color of the flowers. The red maple is essentially dioecious, but this rule is not a hard and fast one, for a branch with staminate flowers can be found on a tree that is pistillate, and pistillate clusters may occur on a tree that is staminate. Examine the flowers closely and one will see that the reddish flowers are the fertile (pistillate) ones and that the orange-colored flowers, fringed with yellow stamens are the sterile (staminate) ones.

If March is mild, the catkins of the alder open, but usually it is not until April that the long, plumed, pendant tassels emerge to wave like pennants. When examined closely they are found to consist of brown and purple scales surmounting a central axis. The scales are set on short stalks, and beneath each scale are three flowers, each having a three- to five-lobed calyx cup and three to five stamens whose anthers are covered with yellow pollen. Pistils seem to be lacking, but if one of the shorter, erect deep-purple catkins is examined, every fleshy scale will be seen to enclose two flowers, each having a pistil with a scarlet style. Hence there are two kinds of catkins on the alder: staminate and pistillate.

In March or April the black willow, the only native willow of treelike proportions in New England, also pushes out catkins—the staminate flowers with three to five long, yellow filamentous stamens; the pistillate with a solitary pistil and two nearly sessile stigmas; the pollen, like that of other willows, yellow and abundant.

The aspens and poplars closely follow the alders and willows, and even accompany them in bringing forth blossoms. The flowers of the aspen occur in catkins that are furry and show a touch of pink. Observe with a lens how the scales of the staminate flowers are deeply cut into three or four linear divisions and are fringed with long, soft, gray hairs. There are six to twelve stamens. The pistillate flowers, found on separate trees, have a two-lobed stigma with an ovary surrounded with a broad, oblique disk.

Except where planted as a shade tree, the eastern cottonwood (poplar) is not common in the Northeast. Like the aspen it is dioecious. The staminate trees are usually densely flowered with catkins three to four inches long and a half inch in diameter. When seen with a lens they are found to contain as many as sixty or even more stamens with large dark red anthers. The pistillate flowers are less numerous and have a somewhat globular ovary surrounded at its base with a cup-shaped disk and three or four greatly dilated or lobed stigmas.

The flowering of trees comes in predictable waves. Though the willows, poplars, elms, and some maples get an early start, blossoming in March or April, the oaks, hickories, birches and a host of other trees wait until May to decorate the landscape with countless blossoms, many of which provide a festive board for bees, butterflies, and a horde of other insects. The staminate flowers of the oak are borne in fringelike catkins, the pistillate in few-flowered clusters. Look briefly at the flowers of the scarlet oak (although any oak will do): The staminate flowers have a bright yellow calyx and yellow anthers; the pistillate involucral scales are reddish, the stigmas a bright red. Perhaps not the most beautiful of flowers but a pleasant surprise when looked at with a lens.

March 30 —
Almost overnight the red maple flowers have burst open — tree is in full view of my living room picture window — a giant bouquet!

Enlarged single flower

Flower — red and gold

A light touch of the pollen-laden flower fringe easily coats my fingers with yellow pollen dust.

Can smell red maple flowers on mild night air —

March 13 —

The signs of spring are present but not always apparent — a seemingly silent rock — an old oak not yet ready to flower and leaf — but spring is on its way, even though it snowed yesterday —

the old oak stands guard before a large snow-covered rock with a den hole under the center at the base. Under the rock in a leafy nest a black bear sleeps with her cubs, almost ready to leave the den. Cubs can be heard.

The hop hornbeam, a lonely forest tree, and its cousin the hornbeam or blue beech, common on the borders of streams and swamps, also bear flowers in catkins. So, too, do the birches. Here again any birch will do if one wants to examine the flowers. I am rather partial to the black birch, perhaps because its inner bark is fragrant and has a pleasant spicy taste, but every birch has something to commend it. The scales of the staminate flowers are bright red-brown above the middle, pale brown below, a color scheme lost to everyone but those with an inquiring nature and a lens in hand. The anthers are of a bright yellow. The colors of the pistillate flowers are somewhat more subdued: The scales are pale green; the styles a pale pink.

The flowers of the hickories, like those of the oaks and birches, are also borne in catkins, the staminate in groups of three, the pistillate in clusters of two to ten. But those of the sycamores, which appear in May, occur in dense heads, the staminate dark-red on axillary peduncles, the pistillate light-green tinged with red on longer terminal peduncles.

The sugar maple blossoms later than its cousins, the silver and red maples; its greenish-yellow flowers in hairy, thick clusters appearing sometime in May. The flowers of the beech also appear during the month, in clusters like those of the maples, the staminate a yellow-green in pendant balls, the pistillate solitary or paired, and surrounded by awl-shaped bractlets.

Willow, poplar, oak, sugar maple, hickory, beech . . . each spring I look forward to watching the sequence of their flowering, in the patterns that shape the season.

Beaver Pond — skunk cabbage up — snow gone — some ice still remains. Beaver's territorial castor scent markers around edge of pond. British soldier lichens guarding a fallen log. Smells good here. Woods full of color for the looking — water high, recent rains. Mood quiet — calm — not all the players here yet — a host of dead trees stand up to their knees in the pond. Red berries on wintergreen. A stump covered with moss, fallen oak leaves, and an acorn cap — rich, lush green mosses — like a tonic to the eyes — I've an impulse to stand here and applaud such beauty except it would interrupt the sound of the wind and water.

Looks to be the remains of a maple.

An old moss-covered, beaver-chewed, tree stump — even as a stump, this "tree" is beautiful as it stands.

APRIL 1, Frog

I have heard the call of the spring peeper issuing from a nearby pond or some woodland pool as early as February, but when I try to trace the source of the call, which is much like a bird's, there's little to show for my pains. At that time of year, with the ponds or pools more or less ice-bound, the peeper remains a mysterious piping voice.

As a boy I would visit my favorite pond in March and scrutinize every leaf and stick and bit of grass, or poke around among the dead leaves and mosses, in an equally futile search. The peeper remains elusive as long as the air is chilly. But in April, when the days have grown warmer and the ponds and pools have become active with life, one should have better luck. Then one hearing the "pe-ep, pe-ep, pe-ep" and looking in the direction whence it came, may be rewarded by seeing a little brown body swim vigorously through the water and then climb up on a floating twig. It's not likely to remain there for very long, but will plunge into the water and swim to the protective cover of floating leaves. Here it will begin to sing, and admirers can then see its swollen throat gleaming like a white bubble. Another peeper may join it in vocalizing, and a third, and fourth, and still others, until many have joined the chorus. Make a noise, however so slight, and at once there is complete silence.

Unless the day is overcast or a light rain is falling, listeners are not apt to hear the little frogs until late in the day or when the sun begins to sink in the western sky. Then they begin to sing in earnest, and throughout the night their high-pitched chorus, reminiscent of sleigh bells, can be heard for half a mile or more.

There is no mistaking the spring peeper. It is small in size, measuring from three quarters of an inch in length, the female being slightly larger, with a V-shaped dark mark between the eyes, an oblique cross on the back, and bars on the legs. In color it varies from a light fawn to a dark brown, the brown sometimes being yellow, red, or ashy in tone. The female is usually light in color. The entire body is delicately translucent, and the underparts are white, washed with yellow, though in the male the throat is brown.

The spring peeper is an inhabitant of open lowland marshes, swamps, meadows, and woodlands, and feeds on worms and small insects, the diet being similar to that of other frogs but simpler.

Peepers begin to mate about the first of April, the males reaching the breeding ponds or pools before the females and always seeming to be more numerous. The eggs are laid singly, never in masses, among leaves and grasses near or on the bottom of shallow water. They are 800 to 1000 in

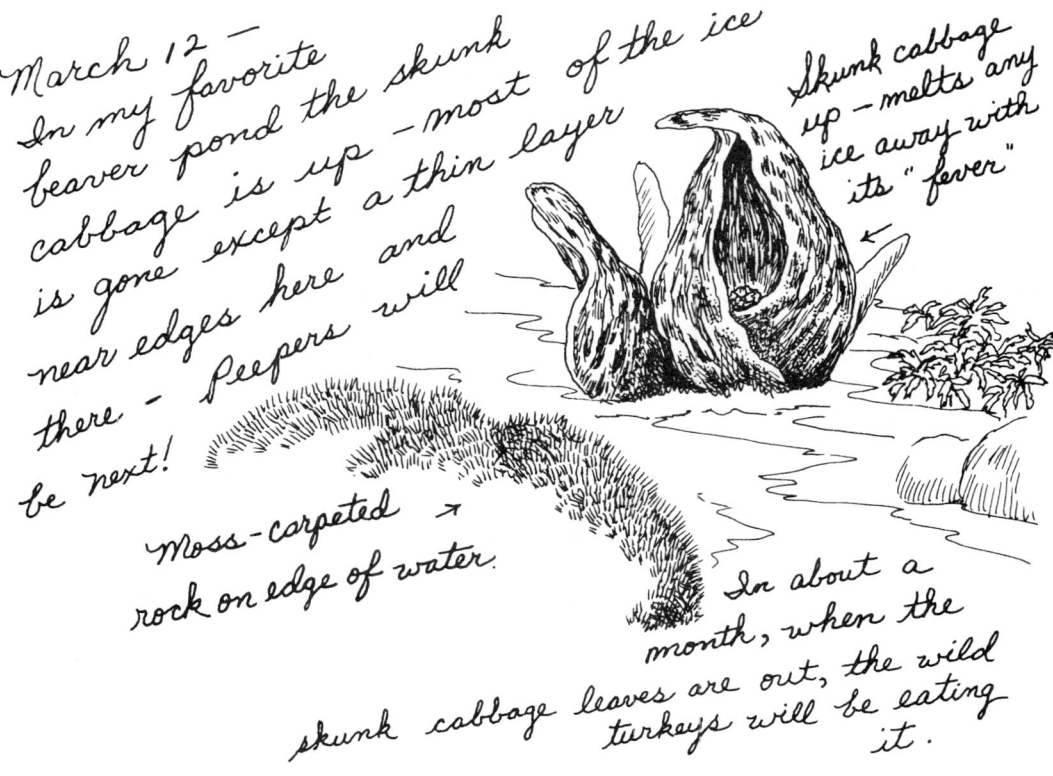

March 12 —
In my favorite beaver pond the skunk cabbage is up — most of the ice is gone except a thin layer near edges here and there — Peepers will be next!

Skunk cabbage up — melts any ice away with its "fever"

Moss-carpeted rock on edge of water.

In about a month, when the skunk cabbage leaves are out, the wild turkeys will be eating it.

number and are white or creamy and black or brownish in color. The young tadpoles begin transforming and coming on land in July when they are little half-inch frogs. The adults leave the water earlier, scattering into moist shadowy places and woodlands where we might find them—if lucky, for they are the most elusive creatures—in all sorts of unexpected places: on tree trunks, in alder or huckleberry, or on tall ferns, but more usually on the ground, among the Virginia creeper or trailing partridge berry, hunting the small insects that seem to be their main interest in life. On a bright sunny day in autumn I have sometimes heard a peeper call, giving voice perhaps for the last time before nestling down under the moss and leaves for its winter sleep.

    The singing of frogs and toads in ponds and marshes is as much a part of spring as the appearance of the first wildflowers, the return of the migratory birds, the emergence of insects from their winter quarters, and the blossoming of the trees. The singing of one species may sound much like that of another, but each species has its distinctive call as well as several other calls. I still remember when I first heard a chorus of wood

March 17 —

Spring peepers calling. Evening at the beaver pond and getting dark fast. Located tree frog easily with beam from flashlight. Picked him up off plant — marking of X clear on his back. So tiny for such a big voice! Usually very hard to find hyla crucifer — only an inch or so in size.

Suction-cup toes for climbing.

Calling pe-ep pe-ep

frogs in a woodland pool and mistook their clucking for the quacking of ducks.

The wood frogs are among the first frogs enticed from hibernating shelters by the spring sun. They follow the spring peepers closely and arrive suddenly, announcing their arrival by a chorus of explosive clucks. Only the males croak and only during the breeding season, but at that time a dozen may croak together in a noisy fashion. While croaking they sprawl in the shallow water or swim about. To see and hear these frogs chorusing one must approach the pool or pond quietly; at the slightest disturbance they stop and disappear. They sing during the day in the pond or pool, and at night too if it is warm enough. The note is very short, a sharp, snappy clack, and at times two, four, or six notes are given in rapid succession; it is a rather grating sound when heard close at hand.

The wood frog is a creature of the woods where its reddish-brown color blends with its surroundings and makes it practically invisible. It is a shy, silent little animal. Its appearance and behavior are in harmony with the delicate mosses and frail ferns that grow in the shade of trees. It seems to be more intelligent than other frogs, and certainly more alert, in hunting the flying and creeping insects that make up its diet. When disturbed it moves quietly from the cover of leaves, seeking escape like other frogs by jumping, but it has the habit of turning so that when it lands it faces the direction in which danger may lie.

The wood frog is a medium-sized species, measuring two to three inches long, with a somewhat flat body, a broad and pointed head, and a skin that is relatively smooth and moist. It varies from light fawn color to dark brown above and is almost pure white below. Its most distinctive mark is a prominent dark brown or blackish cheek patch extending backward from the eye, which makes some people think of it as the frog with the robber's mask.

The call of the leopard frog—the familiar frog of the marshes, ponds, and cattail swamps—is a low guttural note. Who doesn't know the leopard frog? We have all seen it at one time or another because it is the most common of our frogs. It has the habit of wandering during the summer, often some distance from its normal habitat of the pond or marsh. I have met it everywhere, in meadows and fields and orchards, and even in the garden and back yard.

Some say the leopard frog is the most beautiful of frogs. It is rather slender, smooth-skinned, and medium in size, brown or green with a light, raised stripe extending backward from each eye. Between these stripes are two or three rows of irregularly arranged, rounded dark spots with light borders, and similar spots on the sides, which suggest a leopard, though it is also known as the meadow frog and grass frog. Adjacent spots may sometimes run into each other. There is a dark spot on the top of each

Wood frog in the woods —
he is the color of the
leathery old oak leaf
he is sitting on. Had
I not stopped to admire
the polygala — I see
fewer plants each year —
I would have missed
the wood frog.

"Gaywings"
Fringed
polygala

← Purple

← mask

eyelid and a light line along the upper jaw, the underparts being white. The leopard frog varies so much in color and pattern that no two match in every detail.

The leopard frogs assemble in the ponds by the last of April, and their low guttural croaking contrasts with the shrill notes of the peepers and the clacking of the wood frogs. I can hear their croaking until early May and can watch them either by day or by night, as they voice their mating calls. The male frogs, lying half submerged, take a long breath and inflate their vocal sacs, which swell larger and larger as the croak emerges. It is a low guttural note, three or more seconds long, followed by three to six notes, each a second or so in length. However, each frog may ad lib its own solo, following a regular pattern, or giving voice to numerous variations. During the croak the sacs are kept distended, but they suddenly collapse as more air is taken into the lungs.

The leopard and pickerel frogs may be mistaken for one another, for superficially they look much alike. The pickerel frog, however, is browner and the underparts of its body at the posterior end are washed with bright orange as are the hind legs. But the chief distinction is in the shape of the spots, which are more or less square and, unlike those of the leopard frog, not rimmed with white.

The pickerel frog is a species that likes cool water—sphagnum bogs, rocky ravines, and meadow streams—but it may also be found in many other places. During the summer it may be seen in all sizes—from the one-year-old only an inch and a quarter long to those three inches in length—and in almost any grassy place not too far from a brook or pond, where it spends its time hunting insects of various kinds.

From the third week in April to the middle of May the pickerel frog may be seen in large numbers in breeding ponds. Its call is similar to that of the leopard frog but shorter, and somewhat higher pitched, with a distinct snoring quality.

Although the green frog may appear early enough to feed on fairy shrimps in icy March pools, it does not begin to call until May. The call is explosive and once heard is not quickly forgotten. Low-pitched and prolonged, it is likely to be repeated five or six times in succession. One can imitate the call by twanging a rubber band stretched tightly over an open box. Sometimes when given with less than usual force, the call resembles the drumming of a woodpecker.

The green frog is brilliantly green about the head and shoulders but less green elsewhere, the green shading to olive or greenish brown or brown toward the end of the body. The male has a yellow throat. Larger than the other frogs we have mentioned, an adult measures four to five inches long. It may be found wherever there is shallow water—springs, creeks, ditches, and along the edges of ponds and lakes. In many places it

Raining — gray tree frog calling — tame-like. With a flashlight I can get close. Beautiful gold and black eyes. Frog vibrates so fast when calling that it's hard to watch. Call is loud. Picked up — color ashy, mottled, felt cool. Toes sticky. Inside kind legs yellow. I can call him in close by imitating him.

Common gray tree frog

stuck to a poison ivy leaf tonight he is "green" — the color of the leaf.

Still hear gray tree frog — heard him give a short trill from a maple tree. I answered in imitation and engaged him in a little conversation. He has become a talkative neighbor. I wonder what it is we've been saying to each other? "Hello, how are you?" — as I would any neighbor — or is he reminding me, the imitator, that this is his home?

is a frog of brooks and small streams. Follow the bank of a meadow brook on a summer's day and you may suddenly see a green frog jump into the air and drop into the water giving a short high-pitched cry, hence it was once known as the "screaming frog."

Although green frogs may be seen swimming about in ponds and pools from early spring, they do not mate until about the last of May. It is then we begin to hear their explosive calls.

About the last of April or the first of May, we begin to hear the isolated calls of the common tree frog. The call is a loud, resonant trill, ending abruptly. Then about the middle of the month the voices of the males (only the males can sing) are raised in full chorus. They begin calling in the early afternoon, especially on warm, moist days, and continue well into the night. I can still remember the time I visited a pond at night for the first time and with a flashlight spotted a gnomelike male by the water's edge, his vocal sac distended into a small, pearly translucent balloon. He didn't seem to mind the glare of the flashlight and kept right on singing.

The common tree frog is small, measuring about two inches in length, with a rough, warty or granular skin that appears too large for the little animal. Squat and fat, it is an altogether clumsy-looking animal. But far from clumsy, it is actually a skilled acrobat. As it can see small objects at a distance of two feet or more, it will unhesitatingly leap through the air after a fly or mosquito, apparently unconcerned about where it will land. But the tree frog always manages to grasp a plant stem or some support, often with one hand and, swinging with outstretched legs, to pull itself up, blink its eyes, and settle itself comfortably.

Although the colors of the tree frogs are limited to white, gray, green, and brown, they are to a degree changeable. Hence the frog resembles the chameleon but, unlike the chameleon, its color changes are due more to environmental conditions than to emotional disturbances.

I could say a lot of good things about frogs. They seem to me a likable, most appropriate symbol of April moods and longings.

APRIL 5, Jack-in-the-Pulpit

The Indians ate the root of the plant the botanists have named *Arisaema triphyllum*. We know it as the Indian turnip or jack-in-the-pulpit.

Why it is called Indian turnip becomes rather obvious; the root is shaped like a turnip and has a burning, stinging quality, and for this reason everyone should be warned against biting into it. The Indians, of course, knew of this dangerous property, due to the chemical substance calcium oxalate that is present in the root in the form of crystals. The Indians removed these crystals by boiling the roots in water, after which they cooked the roots with venison or ground them into a meal that they then baked into cakes or used as a gruel.

Jack-in-the-pulpit is another name given to this wild relative of the stately calla lily, because some people fancy they see a preacher in his pulpit in the upright spadix overarched by the spathe. At any rate, in the deep and shady woods this quaint little preacher rises in the spring in his parti-colored pulpit, erected beneath leafy cathedral arches, and delivers to the elves and spirits of the woodlands, in a language understood only by them, a sermon as solemn and as profound as any which we mortals might hear in our places of worship.

This early spring flower, that sometimes attains a height of as much as two and a half feet, seems to have a magic charm that makes for wide popularity, for there are few, children as well as grownups, who are not acquainted with it, and few who, as soon as the winter snows have disappeared, don't roam the woods, eagerly searching for its appearance. So well known is the flower that a description seems unnecessary: the novel and beautiful green and purple-brown striped hood (spathe), overshadowed by two long-stemmed tri-parted dull green leaves, and containing within a smooth glossy column (spadix) at the base of which the minute greenish-yellow flowers are grouped; it is familiar to all.

As the flowers are staminate and pistillate on separate plants, fertilization must be effected to a large extent by small insects such as flies and gnats, recently transformed from maggots in mushrooms and rotting logs; indeed the view has been advanced that the plant is possibly developing a dependence upon just such insects for fertilization. It would seem that Jack is an ingrate, for frequently his benefactors, lured to the striped pulpit by the prospect of food, become imprisoned within its narrow compass, and perish miserably. Let us not, however, be too severe with him; on the contrary, whenever we find his pulpit filled with pathetic little corpses, let us attribute their sacrifices to the imperfection of his makeup rather than an intentional desire on his part to play the role of a wolf in sheep's clothing.

The smooth glossy column within the hood eventually becomes a cluster of handsome green berries, which later turns into a brilliant scarlet that attracts hungry woodland rovers who carry the seeds to distant places. Everyone, especially children, should be warned against putting them in the mouth. And we should also add that the same goes for the leaves. Even touching them is apt to produce a dermatitis in susceptible persons.

April 28 —
Today I saw the largest jack-in-the-pulpit plant.

July 20 —
Seeds of jack-in-the-pulpit are green — will turn a bright and shiny scarlet red soon. I raised an orphan crow that sampled the green seeds of jack. It spat them out, shaking its head, and made a coughing sound repeatedly. Burning?

A veery nest on the ground, placed among jack-in-the-pulpit, skunk cabbage and ferns, in the forest.

A barred owl is calling in the distance. Four very blue eggs in nest of weeds, twigs, grapevines, and grass. Left quickly so veery could return to nest.

APRIL 7, Shadblow Tree

The early settlers named it the shadblow or shadbush—though it is more of a tree than a bush—because it flowers at the time that the shad are beginning to ascend the rivers to spawn. Others called it the juneberry, or serviceberry, because its fruit matures in that month.

The shadbush or shadblow is a small tree, fifteen to thirty feet high, with a slender trunk and a narrow rounded or oblong crown of very many small branches and slender branchlets. It is usually found in dry upland woods and on wooded hillsides. When I lived in Massachusetts some years ago a shadbush grew in a roadside thicket opposite my house, and when March drew to a close I would watch for the appearance of its white flowers; they provided a most picturesque scene for the short time they lasted.

The twigs of the shadbush are smooth, light green becoming red brown; its bark is a pale red brown, somewhat smooth or divided by shallow fissures into scaly ridges; its leaves are alternate, toothed, dark green above and paler beneath; and its fruit a globular, berrylike pome, at first bright red then turning to a dark purple with a slight bloom when ripe. The berries, sweet and edible, may be served uncooked as a dessert. They are also excellent for making pies and for canning for winter use—that is, if you can get enough of them; they are not at all abundant and you must get to them before the birds do. Squirrels, chipmunks, and even bears are also fond of them, as are white-tailed deer, raccoon, opossum, and foxes. So there is keen competition for the fruit, an important wildlife food during the early summer.

The shadbush is not a distinctive tree, except perhaps when in flower. Nor is it an assertive one; when the flowers are gone other plants come into life to fill the woods with all kinds of greenery, and the shadbush quite loses its identity. For a brief time, however, its starry blossoms have marked this spring. And I remember them from many springs past.

April 29—
Shad fishing on the Delaware. Broadwing hawks flying lazily north. Pair of pileated woodpeckers at the start of excavating in dead tree high over the river. Just saw a water spout (like a tiny tornado) run across the water's surface—never saw one before. Leaves all lacy green. Shadbush blooming. Caught a shad. Shad migrating up river to spawn. Shadbush blooming and shad fish arrival always seems to be timed perfectly.

Leaves just popping out—flowers first.

APRIL 12, Elm

Like most New England boys of every era, I would eagerly await the arrival of April on the calendar. The nature year was about to begin, and not the least of which, to me at any rate, meant the flowering of the American elm, the first of our native trees to challenge the vagaries of spring weather by opening its small reddish brown flowers. Even in March I would see the flower buds swollen and shining and full of promise, a promise soon to be fulfilled.

For as the sun moves higher in the sky and the air warms up under its benign influence, the buds swell up beyond all endurance; they shake off their brown scales to fall in a tremendous cascade of leaves—for the tiny scales are but leaves in miniature—leaving exposed twenty, tiny reddish-brown blossoms. And then about six weeks later, another shower will cover the ground with little flat, green samaras or winged fruit half an inch long. Wafer thin, they are picked up by every puff of wind to float through the air by the thousands on their gliderlike wings. Flashing in the bright sun they are carried about, perhaps only a few feet, perhaps longer distances, until they eventually land on the ground and germinate into seedlings in some shady or sunny nook, or wherever the moisture content is high. The thought has often occurred to me that whoever has missed seeing the American elm in flower and fruit is much the poorer for it.

Once an ornament on the New England landscape, the American elm towered into the sky like an Etruscan vase and was a familiar sight to those who lived there. Its slender trunk, somewhat swollen at the base, extended upward for some fifteen to thirty feet before dividing into several almost equal branches that diverged slightly as they rose to a height of from fifty to seventy feet; then extending upward and gracefully outward and dividing repeatedly, they formed a broad, round or flat-topped, inversely conical head with branches pendant along the perimeter. This was the tree's ideal architecture and the one I knew so well, when I was young.

June 15 —
Today we cut down our elm. It's been dying for a couple of seasons, and no amount of effort seemed to make a difference — we just couldn't save it. Elm has stood on top of our field so long — a perfect and beautiful tree — an old and familiar friend is gone — Dutch elm disease.

June 17 —
Elm had 48 annual growth rings. Not very old compared with some trees — some rings are quite close — nearer the center — others are farther apart. Widest distance between rings is about ½" — each recording the year's growth.

APRIL 17, Dandelion

To many lawn lovers the dandelion is a noxious weed that mars the beauty of their turf, and with knife in hand, they set out to exterminate it only to find that their efforts will very likely result in an even greater profusion of golden yellow blossoms. (We redouble our efforts with no better success and finally give up with an air of resignation, muttering under our breath that it is one of those things we have to put up with.)

But should one be of a curious mind, and try to discover why such conscientious efforts are to no avail, an astounding tale unfolds, and one learns that the despised dandelion exemplifies, as perhaps no other plant does, the doctrine of the survival of the fittest. Go wherever we will in the civilized world, and we will find the dandelion in almost every inconceivable place, and in almost every month of the year. We may well ask the reason for such unprecedented success in the struggle for existence that every living thing must wage.

Examine the plant and its component parts and the answer becomes evident. Note how deeply the stock root penetrates into the ground—where heat and drought cannot affect it, out of reach of nibbling rabbits, moles, and insect grubs—and breaks through to feast. Watch the winds buffet and bend the stem; though a hollow tube, how strong it must be to avoid harm. As any engineer will tell you, a hollow tube is stronger than a solid one. And why aren't grazing cattle tempted by the rosettes of leaves when other succulent plants are devoured wholesale? Because they secrete bitter, acrid juices.

Examine carefully the golden yellow flower head. We find not one flower but often 300, minute perfect florets, all cooperating to ensure cross-pollination from small bees, wasps, flies, and other insects. They come seeking the nectar (secreted in each little tube) and the abundant pollen, both greatly appreciated, in early spring when food is scarce.

And after flowering the golden head is transformed into a globular, white, airy mass of tiny parachutes, each one a seed ready to sail away on the slightest breeze, to be carried perhaps untold distances before finding a resting place. What is more, each wind-blown seed is able to withstand almost any environmental condition until it has fulfilled its destiny—producing another dandelion plant. Even the briny ocean holds no terror for these tiny travelers; after a month and a journey of a thousand miles they are still able to adapt themselves to conditions as they find them.

The name dandelion, a corruption of the French *dent de lion*, is said to have been given the plant because of the fancied resemblance of the jagged

June 20 —
Some say it makes
a good wine — and
then there's salad
greens to add to
the spring menu.
The sunny yellow
color of the flower is
cheerful. Also, there is
always the sight of a visiting
butterfly to beautify the
plant...
we all know
dandelions'
shortcomings.

leaves to a lion's tooth. It is also believed that the name refers to the yellow flowers that have been likened to the golden teeth of the lion of heraldry.

It is interesting to note in passing that Emerson defined a weed as a "plant whose virtues have not as yet been discovered." But the sprouts of young dandelions have been highly prized as a pot-herb, its tender leaves have been enjoyed as a salad, and its dried roots were used as a substitute for coffee long before Emerson ever saw his first dandelion.

I'll have to keep these facts in mind this spring, as I do battle once again to keep the "lions" from my lawn.

September 26 —
Dandelion seed heads blowing and spreading from one end of my yard... to my neighbors'.

APRIL 20, Grass

Grass is grass, and then some. It covers our lawns and grows in our fields and pastures; certain animals eat it, like the horse and cow. We eat some grasses, too, but know them as cereals: corn, wheat, oats, barley. And one of them, the bamboo, is used as a building material in various countries.

When I first examined the tiny blossoms of the grasses closely with a magnifying glass, I was amazed at their seemingly delicate and fragile quality, and wondered how they can survive the buffetings of wind and rain, or withstand the merciless heat of the summer sun. It doesn't take the soul of an artist or poet to be enchanted by the grace of a swaying grass stem and drooping leaf. There are grasses so tall that they rise above our heads, and others that barely extend above the earth; there are grasses whose flower clusters are barely noticeable, and others whose clusters are a foot or more in length; there are grasses that are stout and robust, and others so slender that their stems are like golden threads. Or the handkerchief of the Lord, as Whitman described grass.

The flowers of the grasses occur in clusters called spikelets, which vary in size and may consist of one, several, or many flowers. The short stem on which the flowers are set is called the rachilla. A grass flowerstalk generally has many spikelets, and collectively they form an inflorescence that may be either a spike or a panicle. A spike is an unbranched flowerstalk to which the spikelets are directly attached; a panicle is one with branches that bear the spikelets. In a spike the lower spikelets bloom first, from below upwards. In a panicle the reverse is true; the uppermost spikelets are the first to bloom, followed successively by those below.

Come fall, the grasses—no less than the flowers and trees—contribute to the autumn color of the landscape, though perhaps less brilliantly. Where the farmer has tilled the ground, the old witch grass lifts its blossoming heads in green shower fountains. Foxtails, both green and yellow, decorate the wayside with their flowering spikes and, in the fields where the autumn sun has turned the smaller grasses a golden brown, the purple love grass spreads a reddish-purple mist above the ground. And about the dooryard, the crabgrasses, the bane of the gardener, extend their spikes like the fingers of a hand.

In shallow water and on muddy shore wild rice, whose seeds were a valuable food of Native Americans, raises its large flowering heads into the sky along the woodland border. The Indian grass attracts attention by its tall stems, its leaves a foot in length. The Cockspur or barnyard grass, with its stems as much as five feet tall and its panicles a foot or more long, invades gardens from its normal habitat in fields and waste places.

We may find too, in shady places about our dwelling, a low slender grass creeping along the ground, with stems two feet long and with slender panicles, which is known by the rather odd name of nimble Will. It is more at home on hillsides and waste places, but I found it in our yard, where I've been doing some grass watching.

May 5 — Canada goose is standing guard over its mate on nest in the grasses. Grass both green and straw colored. It keeps an eye on me, honking disapproval — on nest, appears mate is hiding by extending head out flat on ground in the grasses. Blue flag iris blooming near the water's edge.

Chipmunk in the yard – he is delightful! Sneaking through two-inch-high grass as though he's passing along a jungle path. Periodically sits up to survey all directions – down again to sneak through his jungle – my grass.

MAY 5, Peppermint

Most people are familiar with the taste and odor of peppermint, but few recognize the plant growing along brooksides and ditches and in wet places. Though it is found wild throughout a large part of the country, the peppermint is extensively cultivated for its essential oil, which is obtained from glands in the leaves and used largely in the manufacture of candy. Some people use the leaves for seasoning and grow the plant in their gardens for that purpose.

Spearmint, a European import, has very similar uses, and its oil is distilled from the leaves in the same manner. Served with vinegar, it makes an excellent sauce for roast lamb. Spearmint is nearly always the main character in the mint julep and mint jelly. Our own native mint—the so-called American wild mint—is sometimes grown in gardens for its fragrant odor and pleasing taste.

The mint family consists of some 3000 species; at least a few have popped up in my garden this spring. Superficially, all the members of the family resemble each other. They usually have a square stem with opposite leaves that are covered with tiny glands containing a strong-scented volatile oil of a peppery character. The flowers are usually small, tubular, with an entire or two-lobed upper lip and a three-lobed lower lip, whence is derived the name of the family *Labiatae* (from labiae, the lips). The fruit consists of four one-seeded bony nutlets.

Most people are surprised to learn that many common herbs—thyme, sage, and marjoram, for example—are members of the mint family. Thyme was highly prized by the Romans, and Ovid, Pliny, and Virgil all speak of it. Sage has fewer uses today than it once had, but it is still used to lend an unusual flavor to sausage and poultry dressing. A tea made from the leaves was once used in curing nervous headache, and a mixture of sage and honey is said to be excellent for canker sores in the mouth.

The poor in England often used the leaves of gill-over-the-ground, another mint species, to make tea. Gill-over-the-ground is a small creeping plant common in moist shady places and is one of our earliest wildflowers, the small pale purple blossoms appearing in early April. Oswego tea, a brilliant and showy wildflower whose scarlet red color is strongly relieved by its usual background of shady woodland, is another member of the mint family from whose leaves a tea has been made. The American Indians taught the early colonists how to brew it.

The various species of skullcaps are of interest because, unlike most members of the mint family, these are bitter instead of aromatic. These plants belong to the genus *Scutelleria*, from *scutella*, a dish, an allusion to

April 2 —
Today I noticed my peppermint is through the ground in the garden — green leaves are flat against soil looking like green mint jellies. Leaves when crushed smell strongly of mint. Many more plants are up than were here last summer and fall. I can't resist squeezing and smelling. Day lilies are up about two inches, and pussy willows are green now.

My peppermint plant in summer.

My peppermint plant in spring.

In the fall I dry peppermint leaves on a tray on top of a warm wood stove.

My peppermint plant in winter. →

the peculiar hump on the upper section of the calyx, which, however, does not even remotely resemble a dish. It is a widely scattered genus of blue and violet two-lipped flowers, some small to the point of insignificance, others showy enough for the garden, but all rich in nectar and eagerly sought by bees. One species, the mad-dog skullcap, common in damp and shady places, was used by the old herb doctors to cure rabies, hence its name.

The garden coleus (page 84) is also of the mint family. So, too, are rosemary and sweet lavender, both prized for ages for their aromatic fragrance, as well as salvia or scarlet sage, one of the most brilliant red-flowered plants in cultivation. An unusual feature of this flower is that the calyx and bracts, which are normally green in most flowers, are red, thus making the corolla a brilliant mass of color most pleasing to our eyes and most attractive to pollen-carrying insects. The nectar wells, however, are so deeply hidden as to seem unreachable except by a moth, butterfly, or hummingbird: there is no platform for bees to alight upon and the tube is too long for their tongues. But the bees are able to adapt themselves to various floral structures, and I remember seeing an example of their skill as I watched one entering a salvia blossom. It is a performance that will amply repay a few moments of one's time.

June 3 —

Planted new coleus around the house in the bright sun— for the best colors in the leaves. They are so vivid, provided I pick a sunny spot for them. They rival the other flowers.

MAY 13, Buttercup

Milton called the fifth month of the year "flowery May," and who would dispute that at this time of the year a multitude of flowers appear on the landscape with colors that rival those of the rainbow? Wildflowers appear in the field, meadow, and pasture, along the roadside and in the woods and thickets, by brooks and along ponds and streams, and even in our domesticated gardens and yards.

If there is any flower I can truly associate with May, I think it might be the buttercup, for this association can be traced back to my childhood days, when the bright yellow flowers were a special delight, every child's favorite. And what child of yesteryear did not hold the shining golden blossoms under the chin, as I did, to test one's fondness for butter?

There isn't anything complex about a buttercup's blossom. Five pale yellow sepals—each with a brownish tip and five petals that are pale beneath, but bright yellow above—shine as if they had been varnished and surround the many stamens and several pistils. Each petal is wedge-shaped with its broad outer edge curved to form a cuplike flower. If a petal is removed and examined with a magnifying glass, a small scale can be seen at its base. It covers the nectariferous pit.

Today I looked at a newly opened buttercup blossom and saw the anthers huddled in the center. Later they will form a fringy ring about the pale green pistils, each pistil having a short yellowish stigma. It is interesting to note that the anthers open away from the pistils to prevent self-fertilization, and also that they shed much of their pollen before the stigmas are ready to receive it. The small bees, butterflies, and flowerflies, wasps and beetles too, visit the flowers and serve as agents of cross-fertilization. Later the flowers become a tiny cluster of dry achenes.

We have several species of buttercups, and all have tuberous or fibrous roots and simple or compound leaves that are often cut, lobed, or divided, and have flowers that are prevailingly yellow. The tall buttercup is the common buttercup of the fields and meadows. An immigrant from Europe, it has a hairy branched stem two to three feet tall and deep-green leaves with three to seven stemless divisions that are cleft into several narrow pointed lobes. Both the stem and leaves contain a peculiarly acrid juice that will cause blisters if applied to the skin and is poisonous if eaten. Cattle are aware of the plant's toxic character and shun it.

The bulbous buttercup is also an immigrant from Europe; it is a low and generally more hairy plant than the tall species, is one of the earliest blooming buttercups, and also the most acrid. Also common is the creeping buttercup that spreads by runners to form large patches in fields and meadows. In swamps and low wet grounds I often have seen the swamp buttercup. Its hollow stem is generally smooth but at times may be finely haired. Its deep-green leaves are divided into three leaflets, each with a distinct stem and three lobes, and its deep yellow flowers are fully an inch long.

A May day — Both my sons, when young, were tested by a buttercup — I passed the butter test too as a child. I don't tell anybody, but I still test a buttercup under my chin from time to time....

June 15 —

Picking wild strawberries in my fields. Berries small but good! I've got my nose in beautiful buttercups — they're taller. Eating berries faster than my bucket can get any. Somebody should figure out how to pick strawberries without bending over — easier on the back!

MAY 24, Sunfish

Who doesn't know the pumpkinseed, or perhaps better, the sunfish—also known by other names such as tobacco box, sunny, punky, yellowbelly, flat fish, to name a few. The names given to plants and animals are often descriptive of some particular characteristic; hence the names "pumpkinseed" and "sunfish" are happy choices, the former because the fish resembles a pumpkinseed, and the latter because it is active in the sunshine and more or less retiring when the sky is overcast.

The sunfish is one of the most common and abundant of the fishes in the northern part of its range, which extends from Maine to Minnesota and southward east of the Alleghenies to Florida. It is also one of the most popular, though it is of little economic value because of its small size. I have found it in brooks, small streams, ponds, and lakes, but its preferred habitat is the still, clear water of ponds.

I remember watching some young fishermen at work; they in turn were watching sunfish, on a day in May, like today. Look downward on a sunfish as it swims lazily in the water or in the shadows of the pond bank and it appears a drab olive, but viewed in the bright sunshine and from the side it becomes a rich iridescent blue and green. Spotted with orange and faintly barred with olive, its familiar bright scarlet spot is conspicuous on the edge of the black gill cover. During the breeding season, which is in late May or June, the male becomes more brightly colored than the female, this increase in color intensity being designed to help him in his courtship. First he completes his nest, which is a circular depression or saucerlike basin a foot in diameter and several inches deep that he has excavated in shallow water near the shore; usually in a mass of aquatic vegetation, he fans the gravel away with his tail and pulls or carries away the larger stones with his mouth. He then proceeds to woo some receptive female by displaying himself before her, puffing out his gill covers so that the scarlet spot becomes even more conspicuous and spreading wide his black ventral fins to show off their patent leather finish.

If successful in his wooing, for other males have contested his suit, he and his prospective mate then swim to the nest. They swim round and round with their ventral sides close together while the eggs and sperms are discharged into the water, the eggs falling to the bottom where they become attached to the gravel by a viscid substance that surrounds them. Following the mating act the female swims away, leaving the male to stand guard over the eggs; he defends the nest ferociously against any invader intent on devouring them. But once the eggs have hatched, the male,

Stands rock-still for a long time.

Black plume feathers

Swallows fish head first.

Sunfish

July 11 —
Great blue heron fishing.
Sneaking — raised leg
slowly out of water — feet covered with algae — back
in without a ripple. Leaped
at the water — caught a
sunfish. Swallowed fish
head first immediately. Heron
shook and fluffed up its feathers and
wiggled black head feathers with the
swallowing of the sunfish.

satisfied that he has done his duty, also swims away, leaving his progeny to survive as best they can.

Perhaps the sunfish is not the king of fishes, but try to convince the young angler. For the sunfish has always been the small boy's fish, and through the years no game has brought more joy to novice fishermen. Let us hope it will continue so.

August 3 —
Catching
"sunnies."

Went out on
the lake this
evening — packed a
picnic supper for
all of us. Lake is nice
tonight — sun setting
across the water —
voices of others carry on
still night air — peaceful
fishin'.

MAY 30, Orchid

Today was a good day to go looking for orchids.

Orchids usually conjure up images of exotic tropical forms in the greenhouse. And perhaps rightly so, for these royal members of the plant kingdom are so spectacularly beautiful as to excite anyone's emotions. Moreover they have been so publicized that many of us know only of these orchids, unmindful that there are also orchids growing in the nearby fields and woods. The springtime hiker may know some of them only as wildflowers called *lady's-slippers*, and forgets that they are orchids, too.

Of our native lady's-slippers, the moccasin flower or stemless lady's-slipper is supposed to be the most common. I am not sure it is, since thoughtless people have picked it indiscriminately and it is rapidly vanishing. It would be sad, indeed, if we could no longer find it swinging, balloonlike in the murmuring wind midst the brown carpet of the woodland floor.

A lady's-slipper of bogs and wet meadows, the white lady's-slipper is a handsome plant. And with its flaunted beauty and decorative form the large yellow lady's-slipper of woods and thickets attracts both our eyes and the eyes of bees, though they are doubtless also attracted by its heavy oily fragrance. The similar small lady's-slipper, a delicately fragrant orchid, has a brighter yellow pouch. With the shape of the spurred lip and the sepals around it suggesting a ram's head, the ram's head lady's-slipper is the smallest and rarest of our native slippers. It hides away in inaccessible cold swamps and peat bogs and is not easy to find. Only the most zealous will penetrate the morass in which the ram's head grows for a glimpse of its beauty.

In moist woods we might find the showy true orchids, though they are most frequently found in hemlock groves. This species and another more northern one are known as shinplasters or the small round-leaved orchids, and they are our only true orchids, though there are some seventy more species distributed around the world. Both belong to the genus *Orchis*. Another group of orchids are members of the genus *Habenaria*. It is a large genus of widely distributed species that are commonly called fringed orchids from the beautifully fringed flowers that some have.

One of the more handsome habenarias is the large purple-fringed orchid found in meadows and woods. The smaller purple-fringed orchid grows in wetter grounds. Both are cross-fertilized by moths and butterflies.

Away from the questing eyes of humans in places where the water snake and bittern are at home, grows a beautiful milk-white orchid. To find it, I have had to don hip boots and tempt fate in the muddy waters of bogs

May 11 –
Mother's Day

This mom would feel fortunate to find a rare single wild orchid. Today I happened onto a grove of at least a hundred pink lady's-slippers — all blooming on a hillside under the birches. Were they perhaps ordered for my Mother's Day?

and swamps, for it is in such places that the white-fringed orchid grows. It is a dainty little orchid with a lip that is variously cut and fringed, giving the spike of cream-white flowers a soft, lacelike appearance. Doubtless its color helps the night-flying moths to see it in the dusk. Certainly its long spur is adapted to the sphinx moths. And the yellow flowers of the yellow-fringed orchid of meadows and wet sandy barrens also are beckoning signals to the same moths after darkness, though the butterflies find them by day also.

The orchid family is an enormous group of probably more than 500 genera and somewhere between 7500 and 15,000 species of low, erect, sprawling, or climbing herbs scattered all over the world, but most abundant and most showing in the tropics. They are perennial with bulbous, tuberous, or thickened fleshy stems and roots, with the stems occurring in many varied forms. Most are terrestrial, but there are epiphytic and even some saprophytic species.

Among the smallest of our orchids, the twayblades are often overlooked in their native haunts of moist woods and swamps. These have several species: the heart-leaved twayblade—whose stemless leaves have a shape that reminds us of the ace of spades—and a similar species, the broad-lipped twayblade. Both are visited by small bees and tiny beelike flies.

In Greek mythology, Arethusa was a nymph whom the goddess Diana changed into a fountain so that the infatuated river god, Alpheus—who had fallen in love with her on seeing her at her bath—could no longer pursue her. When Linnaeus came to naming a single-flowered, and delicately scented orchid of bogs, he fancied it as a maiden living in a wet place where presumably none could follow her—thus *Arethusa*, one of the prettier of our orchids. Another orchid of cool peaty bogs and also named after a nymph, the *Calypso*, is equally as elusive. Calopogon, or grass pink, is another of our lovelier bog orchids. The calopogon is not a rare plant, and you can find it rather easily if you venture into the bogs in which it grows. In its company one usually will find the rose pogonia or snakemouth, a delicate little orchid that is far less pretentious than its relative. There are other pogonias such as the nodding pogonia and the whorled pogonia that, unlike the rose pogonia, are woodland plants.

The beautifully marked little leaves of the lesser rattlesnake plantain carpeting the ground beneath spruces and hemlocks of our northern woods attract my eye with their beauty. The downy rattlesnake plantain, found in woodlands generally, is usually a taller plant. The plantains are certainly not glamorous greenhouse orchids, but members of the family nonetheless, and I'm delighted to greet them along the path.

May 25 — Large whorled pogonia is open — three flowers right on forest trail. Across from orchid is trailing arbutus — spring wet and cool this year. Just found five more orchids nearby in bloom! Beautiful, elegant, and exotic-looking. Sepals brownish-purple — very narrow and long.

Green leaves and seed pod 2" to 3"

Purple stem

July 25 — Whorled pogonia after flowering.

Isotria verticillata

JUNE 1, Snake

There was the day many years ago when I happened to walk through an old field marked by abandoned human structures and saw a board lying on the ground. It was pretty much weatherbeaten and from its appearance had been there quite some time. Naturally, as boys are wont to do, I lifted it up to see what was beneath it. Among various archaeological debris I had disturbed a brown snake that apparently made its home under the board's protective covering. The snake quickly disappeared among the grasses, presumably to return to its comfortable abode once I had left the vicinity.

The brown snake—also once known as DeKay's snake, after James Edward DeKay, an early American naturalist—is a most inoffensive animal and so secretive that it may venture right into your back yard without your being aware of it at all. It is rather common in vacant lots where it hides under trash of all kinds especially old linoleum and roofing. In more natural surroundings, such as swamps, woods, and hillsides, it hides under loose stones or flat rocks and under logs or bark, where it spends the daylight hours, coming out late in the afternoon to search for food. It feeds essentially on snails and slugs but, also eats earthworms and various kinds of insect larvae.

The brown snake could just as well be called the "city snake" because it does so often turn up in parks, cemeteries, and vacant lots. A small species seldom exceeding twelve inches in length, this snake is rather quiet in color. It is chestnut or grayish brown with a clay-colored stripe down the middle of its back, bordered more or less with small black spots. The abdomen is pinkish white. There may be snakes more brilliantly colored, but the little brown snake is not entirely unattractive.

When frightened or alarmed it flattens its body and emits a fluid that has a musky odor. It is the only means it has of defending itself.

Snakes have the habit of continually flicking their tongue in and out, as anyone who has watched a live snake knows. The movements of the tongue hold a peculiar fascination for many people, interestingly—and particularly—those who are afraid of snakes and know little about them. Perhaps the reason is that they regard it as an offensive weapon, a sort of stinging organ. Actually the tongue helps the snake to smell.

The sense of smell, as a matter of fact, is well developed in snakes, and many species depend on odor to locate their food. Odor, too, plays an important part in mating, and in many species it enables the sexes to locate each other. This is especially true with the brown snake. During the mating

June 1 —
Found a brown deKay snake in the vetch growing in the grassy field. DeKay has a double row of darker spots that form somewhat of two stripes down center of its back. Otherwise snake is just brown and not too large.

season the females secrete a strong odor from the skin and from glands in the base of the tail. This leaves a trail that the males can easily follow.

Snakes are the only animals able to swallow objects larger than themselves. They are able to do this because of a complex chain of bones that fasten the lower jaw to the skull and which may be moved out sideways. This increases the size of the mouth opening. Then, too, the throat is very elastic. Actually, in swallowing the snake draws itself forward over its prey instead of swallowing by means of a tongue as we do.

Discovered a garter snake at my feet in warm sunny leaves. Picked it up and we looked at each other for a moment or two. It was gentle. While I handled it — so was I!

Feeler or Tongue is red.

garter snake

JUNE 9, Woodpecker

What, after all, do we really know about woodpeckers? The question has often occurred to me as I walk in the woods and listen to their tapping search for insects hidden away in the trunks and branches of the trees. How a woodpecker can unerringly drill into the very spot occupied beneath the bark by an insect is something of a mystery, and, as far as I know, no one yet has come up with an answer.

There are some who believe that the vibrations of the insect as the woodpecker cuts away the wood with its strong jaws are conveyed through the bill and skull to the brain. However this does not explain how it can locate small insects that make no audible sound, or insects that lie dormant and motionless in the winter. Then there are others that believe the woodpecker can fix the exact location of an insect burrow by tapping with its bill in somewhat the same manner that a carpenter, by striking a wall with a hammer, can determine the position of a timber or stud under lathe and plaster.

Woodpeckers are familiar birds, and yet few observers realize how eminently successful they have been in the struggle for survival. Long ago, this family of birds discovered that the female's laying her eggs in a hollow tree or in an excavated cavity would protect the eggs better from elements and predators than would laying them directly on the ground, or in a comparatively frail basket made of twigs, grasses, or other material.

But even earlier in the process of evolution, woodpeckers had become greatly modified in form and structure. These changes assured a constant supply of food in the form of insects that are to be found at all times of the year in burrows and beneath the bark of trees. The woodpecker's short, stout legs and toes, furnished with strong sharp claws for clinging to the bark, are well adapted for climbing. Even its tail of stiff feathers, terminating in sharp spines or quills, can be pressed against the bark as a prop or brace to hold the bird in an upright position while at work. But such equipment would be useless without the means of penetrating the wood and dislodging the insects hidden there. The hard chisel-shaped bill, however, forms an exceptionally effective wood-cutting instrument, and the hard skull is so constructed as to absorb the shock of constant hammering. And for spearing and conveying the insects to the mouth, woodpeckers have a highly specialized tongue that is long and cylindrical, with a tip as hard as horn and with many strong barbs; this tongue is operated by a marvelous mechanism (the hyoid apparatus) that can extend it far beyond the bill. Thus, while most birds must, of necessity, be content with

Rose feathers over bill → *Gray* *Red* ↓

buff ↑ ♀

May 29 – Pair of red-bellied woodpeckers nesting in Stokes Forest. Can hear female (see her too) call from trees, and her mate answers from nest without being seen – just a churring coming from inside a tree! Partridgeberry and wintergreen berries on the vine.

June 28 – Young birds dark eye – head grayish-brown with red flecking. *Light buff*

Red-bellied ♂ calling from inside nest tree to ♀ in woods. Nest hole very round.

Black birch nest tree ↓

Full red crown ↑

June 25 – ♂ Red-belly just arrived at nest with 3 red berries in bill lined up single file. He fed to young singly – backing out each time with one less berry. Can see bill of one young woodpecker accept a berry.

Nearby a brown creeper singing his sweet song. Pair seen nest building in crack behind bark of a dead oak.

November 23 —
Downy woodpecker holding onto the side of dry cornstalks searching for sign of insect life to bore out — very beneficial bird, little downy woodpecker — and a good neighbor.

such insects as they can find on the surface of plants, in open crevices, or flying in the air, or with such seeds and berries as are readily available, the woodpecker is able to find food at any time. . . . And today I was listening to them do just that.

JUNE 12, Red Squirrel

If I again so carelessly venture into an area occupied by the red squirrel, as I did today, I know I will most likely cause the little animal to bark and sputter at me from among the branches while at the same time observing my every move with a suspicious eye. And should I show designs on its storehouse or look into its nest or make the slightest move toward the creature, it would quickly fly into a rage and with convulsive movements stamp its feet and bounce around, all the time scolding me with fury.

The red squirrel is something of a paradox: It is a thief, a nosey parker, unsociable (except during the mating season), jealous (it will ferociously guard and defend domain and food cache), noisy, quarrelsome, mischievous, and insolent. It is also industrious, persevering, thrifty, practical, ingenious, and intelligent. With its keen sense of humor and never-failing good spirits, its jollity seems undiminished by the fierce cold of a northern winter or the blistering heat of summer. This creature is, to be sure, an enigma, and with all its faults, a personable little animal.

The red squirrel is a housebuilder of no mean talents. Its favorite home is a nest in a hollow tree, an impregnable little fort and a dry weatherproof house. If unable to find a suitable cavity, red squirrels will construct a roundish nest of leaves, pine needles, shreds of cedar or other bark, moss, dry grasses and twigs in a whorl of many branches or in a witches' broom usually thirty or more feet above the ground. The nest is ingeniously contrived and surprisingly wind- and rainproof.

This architect also constructs an underground den, usually beneath a tree stump so that it can provide him with a strong roof. The den contains numerous small rooms and a number of passageways. It is surprising that an animal with as much curiosity as the red squirrel should spend as much time underground as it does.

The home range of the red squirrel is limited to some 500 to 700 feet in diameter, beyond which it rarely ventures except perhaps at mating time. Most of its time is spent in the trees gamboling along the trunks and branches with surprising speed and endurance, frequently zooming through the air from one tree to another with leaps of six to eight feet. Red squirrels seem to revel in—and are ideal for—an arboreal life.

With all this dashing about and noisy chatter we may well wonder how it escapes from many enemies: weasel, mink, lynx, bobcat, marten, house cat, hawks, and even big owls—if it is so foolish as to be out at night—to say nothing of man with his rifle and the child with a slingshot.

Most of its food is obtained from succulent growing twigs and buds, various flower parts, and seeds from trees and shrubs. But also included in

Can see a wild turkey hen and her young poults approaching from a distance. I hid in camouflage clothes, in the woods, waiting to get a close look at this wild family. Red squirrel spotted me first. It screamed, chattered, and almost pointed down at me as if to say — here she is! Here she is! Here she is! No turkeys came along.

a good squirrel diet are insects of various kinds: the pupae of moths, hornets, wasps, and bees, the larvae of bark- and wood-boring beetles, plant lice, and occasionally grasshoppers, not to mention young birds and eggs once in a while.

The red squirrel also feeds on strawberries, various kinds of roots, the seeds of grasses, and on a great variety of fungi, many of which are cached where they will dry and be preserved for winter use. How it can eat the poisonous mushrooms that are deadly to humans without suffering any ill effects is something of a mystery. And in spring it is very fond of the sap of such trees as the maples and black birch, lapping it up from a natural break in the bark or making a saucerlike incision in the bark on the upper side of a branch or stripping away the bark to make the sap flow. When it comes to maple syrup, the squirrel and I are in complete accord.

Wild turkey hen meets red squirrel on the back of a tree — both scratching and feeding in same general area. At first squirrel startled hen then she appeared curious — peering at squirrel.

Feathers a little ruffled

JUNE 18, Turtle

Basking on a protruding rock or partially submerged log, and ever alert to plunge into the water upon the approach of danger, real or fancied, the painted terrapin adds a bright note to the June life of our ponds and streams.

It is an amusing sight to come upon three or four of these pretty reptiles sunning themselves on a rock or derelict timber and then, as the sound of my approach reaches them, to see them tumble into the water. As soon as they touch the water, their broadly-webbed feet take an immediate hold and they quickly make for the bottom to hide among the water plants. If I remain in the vicinity and watch quietly for their return, at first only their snouts and eyes appear above the surface. In this manner they will swim about, inspecting the scene for any possible sign of danger, until they are satisfied that all is safe, when they will climb back one by one to their resting place to resume their interrupted sunbath.

The painted terrapin (and its subspecies) is the most common of all our turtles, yet one is not apt to confuse it with any other species. Its olive or blackish upper shell with its yellow-bordered shields (in the eastern painted turtle), and the striking crimson bars and crescents on the marginal shields of both upper and lower surfaces, are characteristics that vividly impress themselves on my memory. Indeed, the painted terrapin is said to be the most beautiful of our turtles and if the above coloration is added to an immaculate lower yellow shell, a head and neck also spotted with yellow, and legs that are marked with crimson lines, we can find little to negate such a pronouncement.

The painted terrapin is found most commonly in ponds and sluggish streams where the flow of water is not rapid and an abundance of aquatic vegetation is available, for it delights to paddle about among the submerged water plants.

But it also frequents marshes, ditches, and similar places. Its food consists principally of plant life but also included in its diet are insects, mollusks, crustaceans, worms, small fish, carrion, and vegetable debris.

The painted terrapin is diurnal (daytime) in habits and is timid and shy in behavior, as is shown by the difficulty in approaching basking individuals without sending them scuttling into the water. When picked up the turtle will sometimes bite viciously but is more often content merely to move its feet vigorously in the air as if swimming, when it may occasionally scratch one's hand.

Unusually long nails arm the forelimbs of the male; he uses these long nails to gently stroke the face of the female during the courtship act, this

April 16 —
Painted turtle "basking" in the sun on a log in the water. Pickerel weed just emerging. →

← Tip brownish
← Green stem
← Yellowish

Water is very dark — moss on part of the log — I dared to look in the turtle's direction and took one step — Splash! It's gone.

amorous feat being accomplished in water while the male swims in front of his mate. The elliptical white eggs are laid in late afternoon in June or July in an excavation made by the female. She sometimes deposits her eggs in a spot a few feet from the pond or stream in which she lives, at other times hundreds of feet from water.

Turtles seem to have a keen sense of hearing, but although they have well-developed middle and inner ears, they are, as a matter of fact, poor of hearing in the accepted meaning of the word. Turtles undoubtedly heard at one time, otherwise they would not have such complete ears, but somewhere in the past they began to substitute other senses for that of hearing. Present-day turtles are exceptionally sensitive to vibrations, and astonishingly slight vibrations transmitted to the skin or shell will evoke an instant response. Turtles have a keen sense of sight and can distinguish various colors. The senses of taste and smell appear weakly developed, though apparently they function well enough to distinguish between different kinds of food both in and out of water.

And turtles have a fair sense of learning ability. Casteel's classic experiment on the painted turtle showed that the animal could learn to distinguish between vertical and horizontal black and white lines and even between lines of different width.

In its native environment, the painted terrapin is active from early spring to October, when it burrows in the mud of ponds and streams and there hibernates until the warm days of returning spring call it forth again. We must add, however, that individuals have been seen swimming beneath the ice in winter. As for me, I enjoy seeing turtles on a perfect day in June.

May 12 —
A bog turtle, very rare and beautiful, basking in a boggy area with a small spring and spring house. Sedges, grasses, moss — very wet here.

← orange

Bog turtle
(C. muhlenbergi)
Older ♀ shell worn smooth — gentle individual.

← Orange splotches or markings on head.

Younger turtles' shells are not smooth — have concentric ridges. Turtle small — about 4 inches long.

JUNE 29, Jewelweed

When I visit the brookside during the summer I know I'll surely find jewels for the asking—jewels of pale and reddish gold and of strange design.

Those of us who are in the habit of roaming about the countryside know the jewelweed well, its exquisite, bright flowers that are pendent from the stems like jewels from a lady's ear. Every summer I manage at least once to visit my favorite brook or the nearest pond merely to catch another glimpse of the flowers that I first saw many years ago. And should the day be a dewy one, I would find that the notched edges of the drooping leaves hang with dewdrops that sparkle like jewels in the sunshine. I have often thought that no other name could describe the plant more fittingly.

We have two species of jewelweed—one with orange-yellow flowers spotted with reddish brown (the spotted jewelweed), the other with paler yellow flowers that are only sparingly dotted if at all (the pale jewelweed). Examine them closely with a magnifying glass or hand lens; observe that they each have four sepals and two petals, one large sepal, in the spotted jewelweed sac-shaped and contracted into a slender incurved spur, but in the pale jewelweed contracted into a short notched but not incurved spur and with two teeth at the apex, the petals cleft into two dissimilar lobes. And to complete this floral picture, jewelweeds have five stamens and a single pistil.

Looking at the long spur of the jewelweed's flower can very well lead us to suspect that it might be admirably adapted to the long bill of the hummingbird, as indeed it is. For beyond the bird's bill, a hummingbird's tongue can be extended out and into and around curves where nectar might be had for the taking, and where few other creatures can reach. The jewelweed, of course, is not the only flower so adapted for the rubythroat hummingbird; first to greet it as this bird arrives from the tropics to spend the summer with us is the early blooming columbine, to be followed by the coral honeysuckle, the scarlet-painted cup, with the jewelweed next in line, and then the trumpet vine and cardinal flower, all of which parade before the hummingbird in a summer sequence to keep it nourished until cooler temperatures send the nectar lovers south again.

To be sure there are other flowers which the hummingbird visits from time to time: the canna, nasturtium, salvia, gladiolus, and others of the so-called "bird flowers" that are mainly dependent on the hummingbird, though insects attend them too. For the shape of the nectar spur is also adapted to insects that have a long flexible sucking tube that can curl around and probe to the bottom. Thus the swallowtail butterflies may often be seen about the flowers as well as various small species of bumblebees. And I should not neglect to mention the large velvety yellow bumblebees, though they do not collect the nectar in the legitimate manner but cut open the nectary sac to get at it.

The showy flowers so familiar to us are not the only flowers that the jewelweed produces. There are also what are called cleistogamous flowers, flowers that never open but which produce seeds, the ripened seeds liberated when the growing seed pod forces open the floral envelope.

Mention of the seed pods leads me to remember another name of the jewelweed, namely the touch-me-not. For touch the fruiting pods when ripe and they will suddenly open to expel the seeds, often to a considerable distance. The observer may be startled at the unexpected volley from the miniature machinegun.

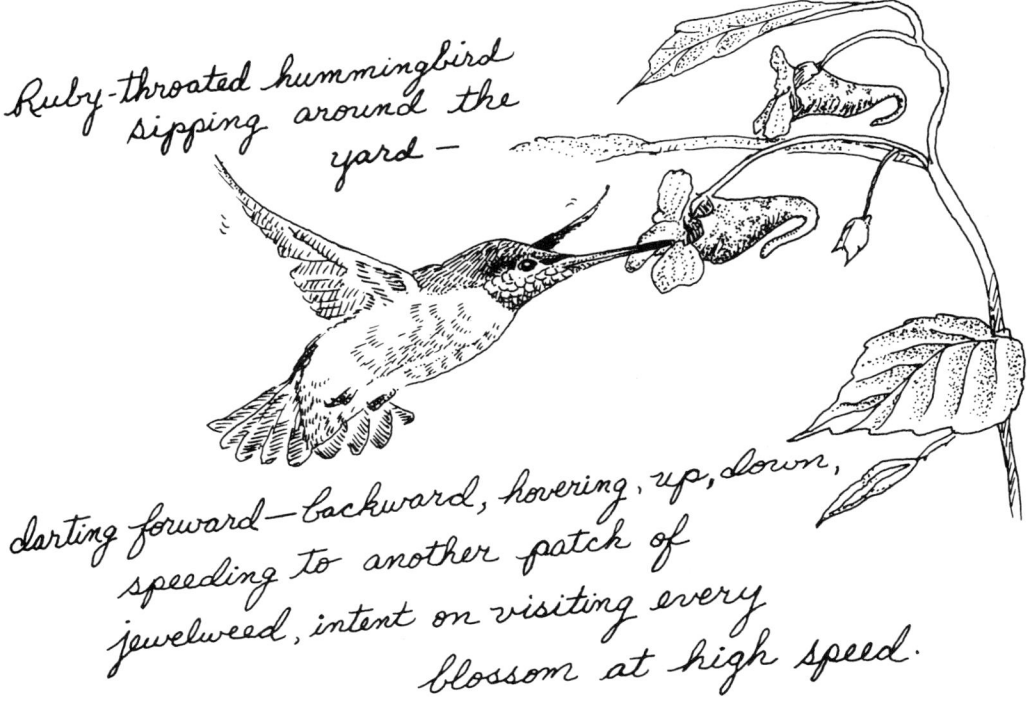

Ruby-throated hummingbird sipping around the yard — darting forward—backward, hovering, up, down, speeding to another patch of jewelweed, intent on visiting every blossom at high speed.

Much jewelweed grows right around the house and fields — thick high clumps.

I love to walk among the blossoms — just to set off the seed pod explosions when they are ready to burst, with a slight "touch."

Pod →

Exploding seed pod.

← Seeds

Also called spotted touch-me-not

May is wonderful. It's one of my favorite months of the year — everything is bursting with bloom. My vegetable garden is doing well — all the plants in neat rows. Found a ladybug in the yard and placed her in the garden where she will feed endlessly on aphids and other harmful insects.

S·U·M·M·E·R

August 13 —
Beginning to notice the purposeful flight of monarch butterflies through the yard and other places. Singly at first — then I see more and more in a day — what a long journey to southern U.S. and Mexico. How do the butterflies who were born here and who have not made the trip to their wintering grounds know the way?

↗ Monarch butterfly on asters

When I was a young boy I found a great deal of joy in watching the butterflies and I spent much time in observing them fly about in the fields, meadows, along the roadsides; many of them even came into our garden. They were a gay, colorful lot and always on the move. It is not surprising they would attract the attention of a small boy who found an interest in the outdoors.

As I grew older my interest in these insects took on greater dimensions, and I began to observe and study them in more detail. During the long New England winter when the butterflies were absent from the scene, I would get books from the local library and pore over them as well as those that my folks would give me to stimulate my curiosity. In time I learned their names and much else about butterflies. I learned which were among the first to reappear in the spring, and I would go afield to look for the early arrivals such as the little gossamer-winged spring azure, one of the first to venture abroad and fly about "like a violet afloat" in search of any early wildflower. Dainty in color and measuring scarcely an inch across its outstretched wings, the spring azure is a creature of many costumes. It seems as if nature could not make up her mind just how to dress this tiny butterfly; over a territory ranging from Labrador to Alaska and south to the Gulf of Mexico, we find one form in one locality, a different one in another.

Another early-appearing butterfly is the tortoise shell or violet tip, which we may also see flying about in the March woods. Or perhaps we might see it on a branch of a sugar maple, sipping the sweet sap from a wound made by a red squirrel fond of the sugary liquid.

As the spring sun rises higher in the sky, other butterflies appear on the scene—the white cabbage, the yellow sulphur, the dusky meadow browns, and the queenly swallowtails, striped and belted with gay colors. And before long they will be joined by the dappled band of fritillaries, variegated by odd dashes and spots of burnished silver; the anglewings with their peacock eyes; the banded and spotted purples; and any others with names redolent of romance and faraway places: the painted lady, the red admiral, the wanderer, the gray comma, the silver-spotted hesperid, the tawny emperor, the hoary elfin.

If one studies them closely, it will be observed that some species visit flowers indiscriminatingly, while others are very selective and visit the blossoms of only a few plant species, perhaps only one or two. But as butterflies are more or less intimately associated with their food plants, I learned as a boy to look for certain species in fields, others in meadows, still others in waste places and along roadsides. I would watch for them along the woodland border, in the woodlands themselves, or in the marsh and swamp. There is a certain amount of overlapping, since butterflies can easily pass from one habitat to another, but usually they stay where they belong.

March 20 — First day of spring, snow still on the ground, but an early butterfly is in the air!

Butterflies also have their own distinctive habits and behavior patterns. Watch an American copper on hot, sunny day and one will see the little butterfly dart at every passing object. Even the pearl crescent chases every shadow. Three or four buckeyes often rise into the air, where they buffet each other about, rising and falling, as they engage in their aerial pugilistics. What a contrast to the lazy, easy-going satyrs and wood nymphs, the purposeful fritillaries, the bustling skippers, the sedate monarch, the vacillating blues that never seem able to make up their minds what to do.

Some butterflies are always hungry and seem perpetually on the move, flying from one blossom to another; others seem less greedy, spending long hours sunning themselves. A few species, such as the little azure, the pearl crescent, the tiger swallowtail, and the sulphurs are as fond of water as the sugared flowers and frequently gather at a roadside puddle, the sulphurs sometimes congregating by the hundreds. I have often seen the sulphurs suddenly rise into the air, flutter about a little, then settle down again.

July 28 —
In the driveway there is a low spot or depression. It holds the water — today several yellow sulphur butterflies are dancing in and around the puddle.

A summer ballet.

What may seem surprising is that some butterfly species are extremely pugnacious, and will chase or drive away from their territory not only other butterflies but other insects and, even more amazing, birds, dogs, and even curious boys. Butterflies have their favorite perches, too, and their own individual resting positions, whether on a leaf, a twig, or on the ground. It is apparent even to a casual observer that they also have their own flight patterns. Watch a monarch and see how effortlessly it sails through the air. Or watch a grass nymph, and observe how weakly it flutters above the grasses, into which it quickly drops if frightened. Or keep your eye on a skipper as it darts erratically about. Just as we can identify many birds at a distance from their manner of flight, we can do the same with the butterflies.

My boyhood interest in butterflies was rekindled yet again several days ago when I saw one of the swallowtails in my garden. The swallowtails (or papilios as they are perhaps better known) are the largest and doubtless the most showy of all our butterflies. The outstanding feature of these insects is their hind wings, which are prolonged into curious taillike projections suggestive of a swallow's. Hence, they are popularly called swallowtails. I might add, however, that we have papilios without tails, which led the American entomologist Lutz to call them "tuxedoes." We also have butterflies with tails that are not papilios.

The best known of our swallowtails is probably the black swallowtail, which is the kind that came into my garden a few days ago. It is a most graceful insect with velvety black wings that have three rows of yellow spots across them. An efficient pollen carrier, it visits flowers frequently, sipping the nectar that they provide as refreshment in return for carrying their pollen.

The female has the uncanny ability of selecting only the plants belonging to the family *Umbelliferae* on which to lay her eggs, for the caterpillars or young will feed on no others. This ability is not, however, restricted to the female of this particular butterfly, for the females of other species have the same gift.

Among the papilios we find that nature has had another of her changeable moods: In the tiger swallowtail we have the strange phenomenon of a butterfly having two or more forms arising from the same set of eggs. In the region north of approximately the fortieth latitude there is but one form of this insect—the familiar yellow and black-striped butterfly which we can often see visiting the apple or lilac blossoms in May and June; but south of this latitude there may be two forms of the female, some females being almost wholly black or dull brownish with the hind wings touched with lines of blue and bordered with crescents of yellow and orange.

The curious part of it all is that out of a lot of eggs laid by the female butterfly, some of the eggs will develop into the usual form and the rest into the black form—both being of the same sex. For many years the two forms were described as separate species, and they were so considered until breeding experiments proved they were the same.

So closely are the members of the family *Pieridae* related to the papilios that lepidopterists often considered the *Pieridae* as a subfamily. The family includes the common white butterfly or cabbage butterfly, one of the first butterflies to appear in the spring. I can see it flying about over fields, meadows, and in my garden sipping the nectar of various early flowers through its long coiled tongue and stopping occasionally to alight upon the leaf of a cabbage plant or some other member of the mustard family, for the purpose of depositing a number of small, pale-yellow eggs that remain attached by a sort of glue. I can still recall distinctly when one of them deposited her eggs on one of our cabbage plants and I was able to follow the life history of the insect in every detail.

The cabbage butterfly is of particular interest. It is one of the few of

September 4 —
A painted lady butterfly —
sitting on a lichen —
covered rock — patterns and
colors
of both
are very
striking and
very alike.

the many imported species for which we have a complete record of the time and place where it was introduced and of its dispersal. This insect—a pest for centuries in Europe where it feeds freely on the leaves of cabbages and turnips—came to our country by way of Quebec during the Civil War and has since spread over practically all of the United States, where it has become established as one of the major pests of our garden crops.

We had our own native species of *Pieris* before the European species appeared on the scene, but like the Indians it yielded its prior claims and retreated before the invader until it is now confined to the wilder parts of our country.

Examine several specimens of the cabbage butterfly and one will likely find that some of them have only one conspicuous black spot on the upper side of each forewing while others have two such black spots. In many insects the sexes may be distinguished by differences in color or in color pattern. In the cabbage butterfly the male has one black spot, the female two. Such differences, known as colorational antigeny, occur among insects in general but are most conspicuous among the butterflies and moths.

Do such sexual differences serve a useful purpose? Probably not. It is doubtful if they have any protective value, but they may in some instances serve as recognition marks, whereby the sexes can locate one another. However, in most instances they are usually so trivial and variable as to be negligible. Furthermore, insects, as far as we know, are unable to perceive colors in the broadest sense.

Cousins several times removed from the cabbage butterfly are the cloudless sulphurs, the common, medium-sized yellow butterfly that adds a distinctive charm to the summer landscape, flitting from flower to flower.

There are many references to this butterfly in the writings of the New England authors, and it was a special favorite of James Russell Lowell who often referred to it in his poems and other writings.

The thistle, one of the most successful plants in the world, found over the whole habitable globe, brings to mind the thistle butterfly, also called the painted lady and the cosmopolite. The thistle is the food plant of this particular "cosmopolitan" species and, as it creeps over the earth, the butterfly follows it. As a result the cosmopolite has become the most widely distributed of all known butterflies.

I like butterfly names. I memorized them when I was a boy, trying to hold their delightful images in my mind. They were as treasured as baseball cards, and that swallowtail visitor in my garden brought the whole collection back to me.

JULY 1, Dragonfly

One summer day when I was ten years old, I was playing in the yard while my mother was hanging up the daily wash. A dragonfly flew in and my mother, seeing it, told me to keep away from it as it had the reputation of sewing up the ears and eyes of bad little boys. I didn't really believe her, but I listened to her and gave the dragonfly a wide berth.

Later I learned that the insect was also known as the "darning needle." It was altogether a myth of course, but it was believed that the insect could even puncture one's skin. But it was a credulous and superstitious age, and all kinds of absurd errors found acceptance. Thus, the dragonflies were also credited with the ability of bringing dead snakes to life and hence were known as snake doctors and snake feeders. They were also known as horse stingers and flying adders. But dragonflies have weathered such slanderous epithets. Today they are regarded more favorably—especially by those who know them well—for they are known to be utterly harmless but of considerable usefulness in controlling various insect pests such as mosquitoes.

The dragonflies are conspicuous members of the water realm, and on a sunny July day they may be seen flying about the shores of our ponds, lakes, and streams, soaring overhead, swooping over the water, or hovering along the shore. Watching these most attractive and interesting insects I have learned that some of them—the larger and stronger—keep to the higher regions above the water, coursing back and forth, passing and repassing the same point at intervals of a few minutes, while the smaller species are less constantly on the wing, usually flying in short sallies from one resting place to another or hovering above the water before they alight. Some of them appear to patrol a regular beat, stopping at the same places like "watchmen at their time clocks." And as I watch them darting here and there, now alighting on a water plant to rest a moment, now streaking off in pursuit of some other flying insect, I might see one of them skim the surface of the water, then suddenly swoop down and touch it. Or I might see another, momentarily poised in the air, descend to the surface in a swift curving movement, then hover above the submerged leaf of a water plant, and then fly quickly upwards, only to descend again to the submerged leaf. Or a third may alight on the stem of a protruding plant rather near the surface of the water and curve its body below it. These dragonflies were merely following their own behavioral patterns; all are females engaged in laying their eggs.

The dragonflies have an ancient lineage, their ancestry extending far back in time to that period when our coal beds were being laid. A fossil

July 2 —
Dragonfly sitting in sun on a fallen log — edge of pond.

Also spotted a kingbird carrying a dragonfly in its bill as it flew by.

White-tailed dragonfly.

← Light bluish tail

July 8 —
Transparent dragonfly perched on a leaf.

← Green darner

forerunner of our present-day dragonflies was discovered in the Coal Measures of Belgium. It was of a tremendous size, having a wingspread of twenty-nine inches. Now *that's* a dragonfly for a ten-year-old lad to be wary of!

The dragonflies belong to a group of insects called the *Odonata*. This name comes from the Greek word meaning a tooth and presumably refers to the strong, sharply toothed jaws with which the insects have been endowed, and which suggests their predatory habits.

Looking at one of the larger dragonflies, some having a wingspread of over seven inches, I can well understand why people of another time regarded them as fearsome creatures for, truth to tell, most of them appear quite ferocious. Their large head and enormous bulging eyes are in themselves enough to frighten anyone timid and superstitious, but they serve the insects well having become thus modified for their predatory mode of existence. The eyes, which often occupy the greater part of the head, each contain from twenty to thirty thousand facets, each representing a visual unit. Often some of the facets are larger than the others, the larger ones presumably meant to distinguish objects seen from below and to the sides, the smaller ones detecting movement. The head is able to rotate freely on a slender neck, thus providing the insects with a greater field of vision.

In addition to the compound eyes, the dragonflies have three simple eyes or *ocelli* and, like other insects, a pair of short, almost stunted antennae that have a minor sensory function; they consist of from five to eight segments, the two basal ones being thick, the others forming a bristlelike organ. The second prominent feature of the head is the mouth or—perhaps more properly speaking—the mouthparts. These consist of an upper lip or *labrum* and a lower lip or *labium* formed of three large lobes; the *labium* and *labrum* nearly enclose the two sets of working jaws, the mandibles and the maxilla, both of which are strongly toothed.

All insects have three body regions, the head, thorax, and abdomen. In the dragonflies the thorax is large and the abdomen long, slender, and more or less cylindrical—well designed to permit the insects to move through the air swiftly and easily. In the male the caudal or tail end is provided with clasping organs used in seizing and holding the female during the mating process. In some species of dragonflies the female has an egg-laying device (ovipositor) with which the eggs are deposited within the leaves and stems of water plants.

The legs of the dragonflies are long and spiny, and are placed near the front of the thorax. They all curve forward and are designed for grasping prey; in flight they are held basketlike to facilitate the capture of flying insects, especially midges and mosquitoes. They are quite unsuited for walking, but in addition to capturing prey they are used chiefly for perching, being adapted for grasping a twig or some other object on which the dragonflies may rest. The victims are often consumed while in flight, but quite often the dragonflies will alight on some perch and eat them at leisure.

The dragonflies are unquestionably the best aerialist of the entire insect tribe, and a glance at their wings will show why. Indeed, it has been said that their flight is almost perfect. The wings, as a rule, are nearly of similar size and are tapered much like those of an airplane. They consist of a parchmentlike or cellophanelike membrane supported by numerous veins of a hard, dark substance called chitin and which cross and crisscross so that the entire surface of the wing is cut up into many small sections called cells. Each wing usually has a notch (nodus) midway along the leading edge, and a distal, pigmented stigma. And needless to say they are controlled by powerful muscles packed within the thorax.

Unlike those of other insects, the wings do not move up and down in unison but beat alternately. Thus, while the forewings move upward, the

June 9 and 10 — Very hot and humid both days — large numbers of dragonflies fill the early evening sky over the field, flying everywhere. Will see green darners soon as they move on migration on the ridge while we watch the hawks, eagles and monarch butterflies doing same.

As hind wings move down

front wings move up.

Head-on

Notch

hindwings move downward, the movement of the wings being so timed that the hindwings do not encounter the turbulence of air created by the forewings but instead move through an undisturbed column of air, the result being that both the forewings and hindwings meet a smoothly streamlined flow of air. All of which makes for a very efficient flight.

Unlike other insects that close up or fold back their wings when at rest, the dragonflies hold their wings out horizontally. And in the early morning, after a cold night's repose, they are at first vibrated in a sort of warming-up exercise before the insects take to the air. On takeoff their flight is at first somewhat erratic and unsteady, but this soon changes to their normal pattern of darting, soaring, and cruising.

Anyone who visits a pond, lake, or stream on a sunny midsummer's day cannot fail to be entranced by the grace and beauty of the dragonflies as they dart here and there among the water plants or fly swiftly back and forth along the shore and over the water. I would like to go visit my favorite pond today, to watch dragonflies.

JULY 4, Birch

The birch is one tree that everyone knows by name, sort of like apple pie and the Fourth of July. Its distinctive white bark makes it conspicuous on the landscape, whether we see the tree sharply etched against the gray skies of winter or outlined against the green backdrop of summer. Today I am remembering birches. I am writing of the birch known as the white birch and also with good reason as the paper birch.

I first became acquainted with the tree as a boy of ten or twelve, while on vacation with my folks who had been invited to spend a few days with friends who lived on a farm in Maine. Needless to say I roamed the countryside at will—but with the admonition not to get lost—and I made what was to me many interesting "discoveries." One of these was the white birch, a stately, handsome tree fairly common on moist hillsides, the borders of streams, lakes, and swamps, and on mountain slopes. It has a somewhat irregular figure, a chalky white trunk, and stout, white, ascending branches that form a broad, open crown. Its bark, cream white and lustrous on the outer surface, bright orange on the inner, separates easily into aromatic papery layers, and is tough, extremely resinous, and durable. The Indians used it and probably still do for making baskets, boxes, as well as for canoes. Thoreau tells us in "The Maine Woods" that the Indians in Maine brewed a tea from its leaves which they seemed to relish.

There are some forty odd species of birches, mostly North American and Asiatic, with one fugitive species found in Tierra del Fuego in South America. They are all medium tall trees with slender branches that are rather erect on young trees and pendulous on older ones. The smooth bark is marked by long, narrow lenticels (breathing pores) and commonly peels in thin papery plates. Because of the presence of resinuous oils, the bark is virtually imperishable and thus is one of the most enduring of all organic substances. The buds form early and are fully grown by midsummer. The leaves vary in outline according to the species, and all have sharp teeth along the margins. Both male and female flowers occur on the same tree and open with or just before the leaves. They lack petals and are borne in a kind of inflorescence known as a catkin, sometimes popularly called a tassel.

The male catkins appear in bud in summer and are either clustered or solitary. In winter they remain erect and rigid, but in early spring they lengthen, droop, and later flower. The female catkins are erect or pendulous and solitary, and when mature form a kind of fruit known as a strobile, which bears tiny, pale chestnut-brown, wind-borne winged nuts.

Took a walk up behind the house in the woods. Carolina wren singing loudly. Nice view from here; I'm quite high. Returning, I noticed birch fungus. In some places it seems to be disintegrating on the trees.

Grows on birch only — can be white to tan in color — grows out of lenticels.

Birch fungus
Polyporus betulinus —
another feature of the birch tree.

The wood of all birches is close-grained with a satiny texture and is capable of taking a fine polish.

Less conspicuous than its more stately relative the white birch, the gray birch is almost as prominent on the landscape due to its white bark—which, unlike that of the white birch, is not easily separated into layers—and to its habit of commonly growing in groups or clusters of several trunks. Another characteristic feature is the presence of a dark triangular patch where a branch extends from the trunk. It is usually found growing in old fields and waste places. Its leaves may be seen to tremble in every passing breeze, their vivid green unusually brilliant in strong sunlight, especially in late spring. Under the autumn sun their coloring of pale green and yellow is no less pleasing to the eye.

Not all birches have white bark: in some species the bark is reddish (red birch), in others it is yellow (yellow birch), and in still others it is blackish (black birch). Of the three, the black birch is probably the best known because at one time birch beer was made from its fermented sweet sap. A sugar was also made from its sap and oil of wintergreen from its inner bark and twigs. For years I have been rather partial to the black birch, a handsome tree whose glossy leaves may be brewed into a delightful tea.

March 17 – 5 A.M. Forest — It's quiet here and a good time to collect thoughts and soak up the stillness of the woods. Morning is the nicest time of day. A ruffed grouse is drumming while a great horned owl hoots softly in the distance — a wild turkey just gobbled – again. Forest waking up. A woodpecker is hammering down near the swamp. Could be a pileated. A crow is cawing.

Ground pine grows all over the forest in this area – yellow birch and tulip tree (poplar). A little brook ambles through. Purple skunk cabbage heads are arranged among the moss and rocks of the brook.

Wild turkey scratchings in the leaves.

Bark curled, peels in curls.

Tree is shiny yellowish color.

← Yellow birch

July 7, Bramble

Adventurous youths who follow the byways of the nature world know the brambles through having encountered their prickly stems, but most of us more fortunately know them by their fruits.

The word *bramble* loosely means any prickly shrub, but the word is commonly applied to the genus *Rubus* of the rose family. They are the blackberries and raspberries and their kin—the dewberries, cloudberries, thimbleberries, and wineberries.

The brambles are a compromise between a perennial herb and a shrub. To be sure their stems are woody, but the stems live for about a year and a half only and then die after bearing fruit, unlike other perennial stems which live for years. Their roots, however, live on indefinitely.

The brambles are shrubs usually bristly or prickly, and are plants with a rambling or arching habit, rarely climbing. Their twigs are usually green or red. Their leaves are alternate, simple or lobed, or more generally compound, the leaflets palmately arranged, that is "finger-fashion." (They are rarely pinnate, or "feather-fashion".) Their flowers are perfect, that is, they have both stamens and pistils. Usually the flowers are white, but they are purplish-pink in a few, usually, showy, with five petals that are often rounded but sometimes small or even wanting, and with many stamens and from several to many pistils.

The fruits of the brambles are known as berries but, botanically, they are not berries. Berries in the botanical sense are fleshy or pulpy fruits that usually do not split open and that have seeds. The tomato, grape, and gooseberry are all berries, and compared with the blackberry and raspberry one can easily see that they are dissimilar. Botanically speaking the blackberry and raspberry are aggregate fruits, or one derived from a single flower with many pistils, and thus are a cluster of small individual fruits. These individual fruits are called drupelets, which are miniature versions of drupes or stone fruits such as the peach or cherry with their soft outsides and single, hard stones within.

Now all hungry hikers know from having eaten both blackberries and raspberries that the former are solid clusters of drupelets whereas the latter are hollow clusters. The reason for this is that in the blackberry (and also in the dewberry) the drupelets are attached to the receptacle (the broadened part of the flower stem to which the floral structures are attached); whereas in the raspberry (including the blackcap) the cluster of drupelets parts from the receptacle when picked, thus leaving the fruit or "berry" hollow. In other words, we eat the receptacle in the blackberry but leave it on the plant in the raspberry.

Cottontail seems to have a favorite nook in the blackberry bushes behind our fence. Last year cottontail rabbit made her nest right next to the house foundation, and it was unknowingly disturbed. When I checked later, the babies were gone. She must have moved her young to a new and secret nursery.

Aside from the fact that blackberries are black and most raspberries are red or yellow, a distinguishing feature between them is that the raspberry canes (as the stems are known) stand erect and reproduce vegetatively from suckers at the base, whereas the blackberry canes arch over and propagate at the tips.

There appears to be considerable doubt as to the origin of the word "raspberry." It is said to have been derived from the Italian *raspo*, meaning rough, in allusion to the roughness of the stems and leaves. Other sources claim that the word comes from "rasp," a wood file. To be sure the "berry" does in a way resemble the surface of a rasp. *Webster's Dictionary* cites the source as the earlier *raspis*, which was a kind of wine, the fruit having much the same taste. Whatever the origin of the word, the raspberry is a gastronomic delight for which we should be thankful.

The brambles are essentially northern temperate plants, but some are found on tropical mountains, in the southern hemisphere, and a few extend to or beyond the Arctic Circle. There are supposed to be from 400 to 500 species, but some authorities recognize twice that number. In addition there are hundreds of varieties and natural and introduced hybrids that are puzzling even to professional botanists. All of which has led to confusion among Latin names and identities, and as a result the genus *Rubus* is in a somewhat chaotic condition. Suffice it to say that a blackberry is still a blackberry and a raspberry is still a raspberry, and both a source of much pleasure when I find them in the woodlands or see them on the table.

From June to August one will find the large showy blossoms—sometimes as much as two inches in diameter—of the purple-flowering raspberry along the wooded roadside, in a thicket by a mountain path, or in a shady dell. The flowers are roselike with five broad petals that are at first a crimson pink but later fade to a magenta pink. In spite of the name, the flowers are at no time a true purple, a color which no member of the rose family is capable of producing. It is a shrubby species with maplelike leaves that sometimes are a foot across. The stems lack prickles, covered instead with red or brown bristly hairs. The fruit is insipid and for this reason is considered inedible, though some persons eat it with enjoyment.

One of the best of our wild fruits is that of the wild red raspberry, found at hillsides and fence rows and the source of most of the red raspberry varieties. It is a somewhat shrubby species, two to five feet tall, with stems having numerous glandular bristles and scattered small hooked prickles. The compound leaves are composed of three to five saw-toothed leaflets that are bright yellow-green above and whitish downy below, and the flowers are white or perhaps a greenish-white about one-half inch across. Only bees and other small insects visit the flowers; larger species are barred by the small erect petals. The fruit, small, red, and juicy, is quite pleasing to the taste, as anyone will agree who has tasted it.

Straggling and prickly, with long arching stems that are often six or eight feet long or more and that take root where their tips touch the ground forming impenetrable thickets, the black raspberry is common along fence rows, by fallen trees, in clearings, and in burnt-over areas. The flowers are similar to those of the wild red raspberry but are sparingly visited by insects. The fruit is purplish-black and considered by some to be superior to that of the wild red raspberry.

The plant commonly called the brier is otherwise known as the high-bush blackberry. Most of us are familiar with it as it springs up in neglected places and if unmolested soon takes possession.

We find it along the seashore, on the mountainside, on the woodland border, by the roadside, in a burnt-over field, and along the fence row; it's an adaptable plant tolerant of varying conditions.

The high-bush blackberry is a straggling prickly shrub with both erect and recurved stems three to eight or nine feet high. The leaves are composed of three or five ovate or egg-shaped leaflets, and the white flowers, about an inch across, are borne in terminal racemose panicles. The flowers of the blackberries are constructed to permit visits by such insects as the heavy bumblebees, with larger petals that are spread out flat, the better to attract them.

Those who have picked the fruit of the tall blackberry know that this fruit (from half an inch to an inch long) varies considerably. Thus some of the "berries" may be large, others small; some may be sweet, others sour; and some plants may produce an abundance of fruit whereas others may provide only a meager supply.

Lastly, let me say a few words about the dewberry, also known as the creeping or running blackberry. The latter name is quite descriptive of the plant, for it trails its woody stems along the ground for several feet. We find it along the roadsides, in fields, and on rocky hillsides. Walt Whitman once wrote that the "berries" are flavorous and juicy. To be sure they are of large size and excellent flavor, but unfortunately there are never enough of them for the stroller with a longing for a sweet. And brambles or no, today is a good day for berry picking.

July 19 —
Blackberries everywhere — every outside chore takes me past the berries, and I pick and eat as I go. Why is it the berries on my bushes are smaller than my neighbors' across the road? Or does it just look that way?

JULY 10, Queen Anne's Lace

One of the more familiar wildflowers of the summer landscape is the ubiquitous Queen Anne's lace (also known as the wild carrot and bird's nest) that we see growing in fields and meadows, along the roadside, and in waste places. A plant from one to three feet high with lacy, flat-topped clusters of tiny cream-white flowers, it is most effective in catching the eye. Especially now, in the heart of July.

One would have to examine the lacy flower clusters with a magnifying glass or hand lens to appreciate their delicate structure and perfection of detail. The small white flowers are disposed in a radiating pattern like a handmade piece of lace, and in the very center of each cluster there is a tiny purple floret that is not a part of any of the smaller clusters but is set upon its own isolated stalk. As far as I know, no one as yet has been able to explain this construction; it is one of those mysteries that we meet with now and then.

April 6 — Found a hawk feather caught in the dead Queen Anne's lace from winter. Weed still standing on the edge of an old field. The familiar "bird nest" appearance of the winter stalk.

It is said that over sixty different species of insects may be taken from the flat-topped flower clusters. This is because the flowers secrete a considerable amount of nectar that is easy to reach. Even the shortest-tongued insects can sip the nectar in less time than it takes to sip from the tubular florets of the *Compositae,* which accounts in part for the plant's wide distribution. When the flowers have served their purpose, the entire cluster dries and curls up in the form of a bird's nest.

The wild carrot was once believed to be the progenitor of the cultivated carrot but its long tapering root lacks the sweetness of the garden variety. All attempts to produce an edible root from the wild one have failed; moreover, if the cultivation of the garden variety is allowed to lapse for a few generations, it reverts to the ancestral type, which is quite distinct from the wild carrot.

August 1 —
Queen Anne's lace is so thick over the top of deep green field it looks as if nature has spread her best lace tablecloth over my pasture. I imagine that's how it might appear from higher bird's-eye view. The table is set. Seeds, insects, and other tasty morsels abound in the grassy field for the taking.

JULY 14, Flying Squirrel

Some years ago I received a letter from a correspondent asking how to get rid of a family of flying squirrels that had taken possession of her attic.

They are delightful little animals, and a joy even in the house if properly confined. But I could sympathize with her; unrestrained, they can prove quite a nuisance. It doesn't take much imagination to picture them in her attic, chasing each other, squealing and scratching and up to all sorts of high jinks.

Flying squirrels do not often get into a house for they are essentially woodland animals and seldom venture far from that habitat. Indeed, though they may be abundant in the woods near my house, I would probably not know they were there because they sleep during the daylight hours and are about only at night.

They live in holes in trees, but if suitable holes are not available they make a nest of leaves and bark high in the branches. Sometimes one can arouse them by rapping on the trees and occasionally get them to "fly." But more likely they will emerge from their nest and then go right back to sleep, clinging to the bark like lichens and looking for all the world like some fungus growth.

If the naturalist wants to see flying squirrels at play he or she must forego part of a night's sleep, but these beautiful little forest folk are worth it. Find a comfortable seat in the woods on a bright moonlight night in July and be quiet and patient. The observer may have to wait for what seems like hours. Suddenly there's a slight rustle among the leaves overhead, and the next moment one might see a shadowy form glide swiftly through the air and alight on the bole of a tree. Then another comes sailing after it, then another, and still another, until the night air seems full of them.

The squirrels glide through the air on loose folds of skin that extend along each side from wrist to ankle. These folds stretch out when the squirrels spread their legs and, supported by these folds, they glide in a long graceful sweep from high on one tree to the base of another. The tail acts as a sort of rudder and helps them to make a four-point landing. It also prevents them from dashing their brains out when landing.

Flying squirrels are sociable little animals and tend to live in groups. They are extremely timid and shy of humans, however, and when caught appear terror-stricken and paralyzed with fear. Even when roughly handled they will not use tooth and claw in an effort to escape as most other animals do.

Tail flat, rudder-like →

Extra skin stretched out between legs, → kite-like

↑
Large eye, nocturnal squirrel

July 4 — 9 A.M. Curiously knocked on tree with hole near the top. A flying squirrel appeared in opening and took flight. Glided downward to nearest tree trunk, landed and scampered up again. Surprise!

Walked the dog about 9:30 P.M. and noticed a movement on the bird feeder. Two flying squirrels!

Moving slow, trying not to scare them — could watch closely. They did not run away.

Hand fed squirrels some peanuts. They liked bread too — How many nights have you two visited my feeder for seed?

JULY 16, Mushroom

Years ago when I lived in Massachusetts I belonged to a mycological club. During the warmer months of the year we would take field trips, and before returning home we would build a fire and cook the edible mushrooms that we had collected and serve them in melted butter on toast. They were a gourmet's delight. Of course we had to *know* our mushrooms, and we did.

Although mushrooms of one kind or another are to be found at almost any time of the year, they occur in the greatest abundance during the months of July, August, and September, and like the flowering plants each species has its own growing season. Among the first to appear in the spring is the glistening coprinus and the sponge mushroom, the latter one of the most sought after. These in turn are followed by the shapely little brownie cap, the hedgehog mushroom, the uncertain hypholoma—its white fragile cap quite conspicuous among the grasses of a lawn—the waxy laccaria with its reddish cap, and (after a few days of rainy weather) the fairy-ring mushroom in odd ringlike formations.

Mushrooms, rather unusual plants, have always had a peculiar fascination for me. In the popular mind the term "mushroom" seems to be limited to a single species, the one we buy in the stores, while those that are found growing in the wild are generally referred to as "toadstools." But a toadstool is a mushroom and a mushroom is a toadstool, for botanically they are alike.

As spring passes into summer the mushrooms become more numerous: the meadow mushroom, the species cultivated to serve as food; the common naucoria, in pastures and on our lawns, its homogeneous brownish colors making it fairly easy to identify; the bell-shaped panaeolus of a peculiar leaden tint; and the haymaker's mushroom, one of the more common of our mushrooms and also one of the easiest to recognize with its conic, smoky-brown cap.

But these are only a few; there are others such as the sheathed amanitopsis of somewhat variable color; the beautiful yellow chanterelle; the vermilion mushroom, often of a deep red; the oak-loving mushroom, equally at home in a pasture and in a woodland grove; and the scaly lentinus, the train wrecker, so named from one of its habits of growing on railroad ties and destroying them by so doing. And, of course, we must mention the tall, stately destroying angel, its shimmering, satiny whiteness symbolic of innocence, but one of the most poisonous mushrooms known. Nor should we forget the equally deadly fly amanita; the beautiful

Jack-o-lantern, which will emit a soft greenish light if you place it in a dark room; the dainty coral mushroom; and the green and red russalas that rival the higher flowers in the brilliance of their coloring.

And if one follows the byways of the nature world at this time of the year, sure to be seen are the perplexing hypholoma growing in dense clusters; the sharp-scaled pholiota; perhaps the oyster mushroom jutting out from the trunk of a tree; and most surely we will be entranced with the delicate, violet-tinged beauty of the masked tricoloma.

April 28 —
Morels are up again under the spruce trees. We picked them, washed and sliced them for cooking with steak — a gourmet's treat. Only seem to see them under my spruces and in very few numbers. They come up quickly and disappear quickly. Freeze well for later cooking.

← Tan mushrooms

← Whitish stem

Giant white puffball ↓

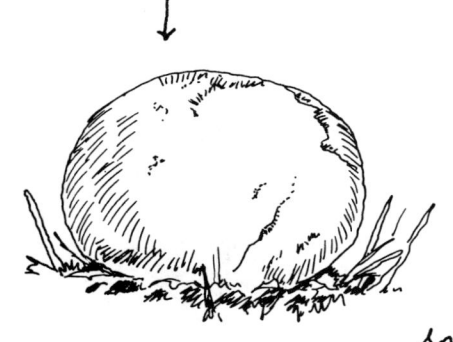

April 16 — Dried-looking puffballs — 3 under spruce trees. When I squeezed them, spores puffed out the hole. In summer found giant white puffball that I've washed, and sliced like bread and browned in butter.

Brownish puffballs ↑

JULY 21, Waterlily

It is a long time since I read Longfellow's *Hiawatha*, yet a few lines remain in my memory. Whenever I see the yellow waterlily I remember that it was Hiawatha's canoe that "Floated on the river . . . Like a yellow water lily."

There is much to be said in praise of the yellow waterlily, although unlike its cousin the white waterlily it has no fragrance. The white lily's white, golden-centered chalices perfume the air with their delicious fragrance and attract bees, flowerflies, and other insects, which must visit the flowers in the morning, since they close in early afternoon.

The hiker or pond watcher is likely to look at a rich green lily pad and fail to grasp the practicality of its leathery and waterproof design. It can withstand not only heavy rain, but the wear and tear of wavelets that often toss it about like a raft in an angry sea. It also serves as a hatchery for eggs of many kinds, and as a pasturage for the larvae of insects and snails. Sometimes bryozoans find it a convenient place to locate their colonies.

The yellow pond lily is also known as the cow lily, bullhead lily, or spatterdock. It is common in standing water, ponds, and slow streams, and often grows in densely populated shallows, where water striders skate about on what little water there may be, numberless springtails form gray-black patches on the surface, and whirligig beetles come venturing in from open water. The yellow pond lily has oval or heart-shaped leaves, with long stems rising from thick root stalks that creep in the mud. The green and yellow, cup-shaped flowers have six fleshy sepals that resemble petals. The true petals are stamenlike, oblong, fleshy, short, and yield nectar. When the flower first opens, there is a triangular opening over the stigma that is so small that an entering insect must come in contact with it. The next day the flower expands fully, and the anthers beneath the stigma unfold, spread outward, and expose the pollen, thus ensuring cross-pollination. The mining bees of the tribe *halictus* are the chief agents in the transfer of pollen, though the mining bees of the tribe *andrena* and various flies also transport the pollen.

On any bright summer day beetles of the genus *Donacia* may be seen walking over the lily pads, flying into the air, then returning to them, their metallic green, bronze, or purple bodies gleaming in the sunshine in sharp contrast to the dark green of the leaves. Frequently the leaves are riddled with holes where they have laid their eggs.

Unlike the yellow pond lily, the white waterlily, found in still waters everywhere, is fragrant. Its leaves are roundish, leathery, thick, purplish-red beneath and dark green above. The flowers are white, often five inches in diameter, open in the morning, and close at noon. The sepals are green, tinged with reddish-brown, the petals broadly lance-shaped, and the golden stamens are many, the outermost becoming petallike and white. Bees and flowerflies are the chief visitors, but beetles and butterflies attend the flowers also. In both species, the fruit is berrylike, with that of the white waterlily maturing beneath the surface of the water, and that of the golden pond lily above. Both of them are to me the essence of July.

Yellow bullhead-lily

July 12 —
Yellow water lilies and frogs — grazing dairy cows on the banks of the lazy pond — a farmer's son fishing — a summer day.

May 4 —

Wild calla lily blooming in the water on edge of beaver pond. A green heron is feeding down the brook. The lily is beautiful — large green leaf. Flower on a short spike — nestled inside a single petal. A small group of plants in a very wet area. Wonderful wild lilies (aquatic flower).

Greenish-white petal

Flower

Green leaf

JULY 25, Toad

Shakespeare was wrong on two counts. The toad is not venomous, and it does not wear a jewel in its head.

Many of us, in this age of enlightenment, still cling to myths and beliefs that long since have proven false. For instance, many people today still believe that toads are cold and slimy to the touch and that they are loathsome because they live in dark and damp places—in other words, that no self-respecting animal would live in such a place.

It is true that they are sometimes cold to the touch, but they can also be very warm. The reason for this is that the toad is cold-blooded, and hence its body temperature changes with that of its environment. On a warm, sunny day the toad might be very warm indeed, and conversely on a cold day it could be very cold, so cold that it might dig down in the earth and sleep all day. As for being slimy, however, the toad is on the contrary normally very dry. To be sure, if one squeezes it a little too hard or handles it somewhat roughly a toad will become slightly wet, but this is a defensive measure. The fluid that it secretes at such times is colorless and odorless and quite harmless. The toad, however, is also able to secrete another fluid—when in great agony—that is slightly poisonous. This fluid is secreted by the skin and is especially abundant in the parotoid glands, the two large swellings behind the eyes. The toad usually reserves this defensive weapon for times when it is seized by the teeth of an enemy, for the fluid has a disagreeable effect on the mucous membrane of the mouth. I have seen more than one dog drop a toad in a hurry.

The toad selects a cool, moist place in which to spend the day. This is not only for the shelter which such a place provides, but more important for its moisture content. A toad does not drink water in the ordinary way but absorbs it through its skin. Keep a toad in a dry place and it will soon become thin and depressed looking. Within a few days it will probably die. But provide it with plenty of moisture and it will remain plump and contented, even though it may not get much food.

Now just because a toad does not drink in the ordinary way, is no reason why it does not enjoy drinking. Watch how it sprawls out in shallow water or on a wet surface, and with what apparent enjoyment it literally "soaks" in the water.

Toads are not without a certain beauty. Their eyes, especially, are brilliant and beautiful. In the past this beauty gave rise to the fable that the toad has a jewel in its head. This jewel was supposed to be a precious stone, and when worn as a talisman was believed to protect the wearer from all sorts of evil.

August 2 —
American toad sits on my doorstep — or is it his doorstep — almost every night in the light of the window for the opportunity to catch insect meals in the nearby garden. It's very docile, and I can easily pick him up and look at him.

I'm aware of this toad underfoot every night when I go out. I step carefully — he sits anywhere he wants to — on his doorstep.

Beautiful gold eyes →

As the summer afternoon begins to wane, the toad leaves its snug retreat and begins its nightly search for food. I can see them on night patrol on my lawn. The toad will eat almost any small living thing that is abroad during the hours of darkness: flies, beetles, grubs, caterpillars, crickets, grasshoppers, tree hoppers, ants, plant lice, army worms, spiders, sow bugs, earthworms, and the like. To watch a toad hunt is well worth a few moments of anyone's time. Observe how still it sits, its head bent slightly forward, its eyes bright with anticipation. A fly alights within two inches of its nose. The toad opens its mouth and the fly is gone. So quickly does the toad thrust out its tongue, to which the fly adheres and is carried far back into its mouth, that we are hardly aware of what has happened.

Some years ago it was found that about 88 percent of a toad's food consists of insects and other small creatures that are considered pests in the garden. It was estimated that in *three* months a toad will eat some 10,000 injurious insects (of this number 16 percent are cutworms, 9 percent caterpillars, and 19 percent weevils and other injurious beetles). At that time a toad was valued at $19.44 for the cutworm alone it devours in a single season. At our present inflationary rates who knows what a toad is worth?

Toad's tongue is attached to the front of his mouth, not the back.

August 4 — American toad feeding in my garden at night.

Sticky surface — and when it is flung out of back of mouth an insect is stuck on tongue and pulled back into mouth — quick as a wink.

JULY 31, Loon

It came as my wife and I were putting away the supper dishes in our cabin. At first a soft sibilant sound, it suddenly exploded in a wild maniacal laugh. It broke the silence of the Maine woods with such unexpected suddenness that both my wife and I were terrified, never having heard it before. But then gradually regaining my composure I realized what it was; we had just heard the voice of the loon.

It so happened that our July stay in the Maine woods those many years ago was the first of many visits that followed through the years. But I have never forgotten the experience. As the evening wore on I decided that the next day I would visit the nearest pond in the hopes of seeing the bird itself. I was lucky that next morning: I saw the bird swimming not too far from the shore, now and then diving for his breakfast of a fish or two.

The loon is about the size of a small goose, black and white and unmistakable in summer, with a long black daggerlike bill used expertly in spearing fish and crustaceans, and large webbed feet that it employs to good advantage in swimming.

There are two features about the loon that command our attention: its calls and its phenomenal ability to dive and to swim underwater for a long time. On land the loon is a clumsy awkward traveler, especially when in a hurry, when it flounders forward using both wings and feet. And strangely enough it has great difficulty in taking to wing. But once in the air it is the personification of motion in flight.

The bird is the most remarkable and powerful example of avian mechanics ever devised for flying the stormy seas of the New England coast. It will fly straight ahead in the teeth of a gale and then, slanting suddenly downward and just beyond the top of a towering wave, will shoot down its surface and then rise again on the coming crest. With the seas running high and the wintry gales whipping the spray from their white tops in cloudy gusts, the loon finds a quiet bay and will rest at ease like a ship at anchor.

Legs and feet position of loon – very far to rear of body – loon more at home in water swimming than on land walking.

Vacationing at the St. Lawrence River. Doing a lot of fishing. Back in the reeds, in a quiet cove of the bay, our boat rounded a bend and we surprised a loon on the nest. What a thrill — eggs in nest — left quickly so the loon would come back.

Nest is a pile of wet-looking reeds in a wet area.

AUGUST 3, Whippoorwill

On a summer's night I often sit on my porch and read, the quiet of the night often broken by the sweet notes of the whippoorwill in the distance. Few people have ever seen the whippoorwill, though I doubt if there are many birds more widely known. The answer to this seeming paradox is the bird's call, which is as familiar as the caw of the crow. Yet it is so rarely seen because of its coloration, which so blends with the ground and the fallen leaves and twigs that it becomes practically invisible. Even one with a keen trained eye might search for it for thirty minutes or more before detecting its outline. Once flushed the bird will fly rapidly and noiselessly for a short distance and then suddenly plunge to the ground, where it disappears as if the ground had opened up and swallowed it.

It is natural for us to suspect anything that moves about in the dark; since the beginning of recorded time man has feared the evil that stalks about at night. But an animal as harmless as the whippoorwill should never be regarded with suspicion or alarm. Whenever one of these birds appears about our dwelling it should be greeted as a welcome visitor because of the many insects it destroys.

When the birds have mated, the female selects some remote spot in the woods or beneath dense shrubbery and as a rule deposits her eggs on the dead leaves that usually cover the ground in such places. If the female bird is not molested or disturbed the young are hatched and reared in the same spot.

Audubon heard the whippoorwill, and he wrote:

> Immediately after their springtime arrival their notes are heard in the dusk and through the evening in all the thickets and along the edge of the woods. Clear and loud, they are to me more interesting than those of the Nightingale. I have probably acquired this taste by listening to the Whippoorwill in places where nature's beauty and solitude are grandest. You can think how grateful I have been for the cheering voice of this my only companion when, fatigued and hungry after a day of unremitting toil, I have pitched camp in the wilderness as darkness put a stop to my labors.

I share Audubon's pleasure in the company of a whippoorwill, when one joins me somewhere near my porch on an August evening.

Was that the call of the whip-poor-will? Yes — loud and clear — calling from the woods. I rarely see the whip-poor-will. But tonight over and over it calls its name. It's getting dark — time to go.

AUGUST 5, Cattail

Driving through the countryside today I caught a glimpse of the phalanx of cattails in the distance, each standing as a silent sentinel over the marsh and each with a red-brown spike silhouetted against the sky.

Cattails are a familiar feature of the landscape at this time of the year. Most of us usually pay them scant attention, though they deserve more than a passing notice for the important role they play in the ecology of the wetlands. Their extensive rooting system serves to retard the runoff of large quantities of water and is very important in flood control. They have creeping rootstalks that grow in all directions. In a few years each parent plant becomes the center of a colony that may be several acres in extent. These rootstalks are natural root cellars and store up foods manufactured by the leaves during the summer, which are used to promote the sprouting and growth of new plants in the spring. Geese and muskrats feed on the starchy rootstalks, and at one time the Indians dried and ground them into a meal. It is said that the early settlers of Virginia were exceptionally fond of them. Even today people who are in the habit of gathering wild plants for food use cattail root in various ways and claim it tastes much like a potato.

As the spring sun begins to warm the landscape and the water of the marsh rises in temperature, new plants gradually arise from the underground rootstalks, with their bright green a delightful contrast to the sombre colors of the winter marsh. The bannerlike leaves of the cattail are long and ribbonlike, smooth, strong, olive green, and flexible so that they yield to the wind instead of defying it. The Indians harvested and dried the leaves and used them in making baskets and waterproof mats. Even today they are used in making the rush seats to be found in some wooden chairs.

As spring gradually passes into summer the cattails begin to flower, and the tips of their cylindrical heads may be seen to be covered with a fine drooping fringe of olive yellow. When examined closely with a magnifying glass or hand lens, the yellow is seen to be a mass of crowded anthers packed with pollen. This pollen (which is yellow and edible and was used as a partial substitute for wheat flour in the making of golden "Indian breads") falls on the pistillate flowers below on the same flower stalks, or with every passing breeze is carried to neighboring flowers. It is virtually useless to look for the pistillate flowers; lacking both petals and sepals and covered with a down, they are hidden from view. Even with the aid of a magnifying glass, they are difficult to find. It is the down, of course, that forms the familiar cattail of late summer or early fall. The brown heads of the spikes contain innumerable closely packed nutlets, each with a number of fluffy hairs that serve as a parachute to carry them to near and distant places, where, if they fall on a mudflat, they will germinate the following spring. It has been estimated that in a dense cattail marsh, billions of viable seeds may be produced in a single year. As with the other parts of the cattail, the fluffy hairs have been found useful for stuffing pillows and mattresses, and, in the Second World War, for filling liferafts and life preservers.

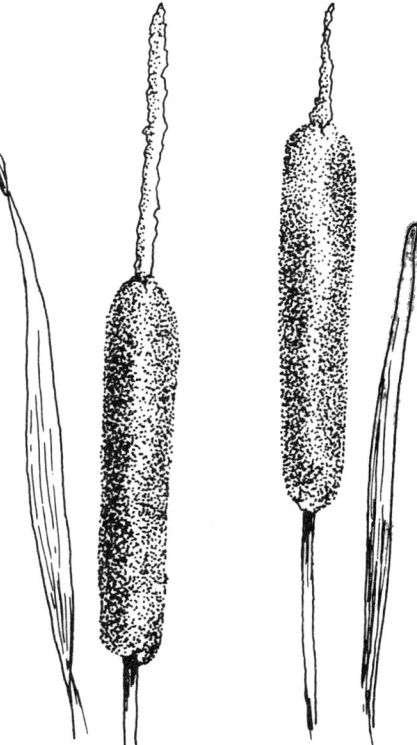

New cattails in the marsh — when I was young I picked new cattails to burn. Dried, they smoldered and we believed no mosquito would nibble on the person holding a burning cattail. I can still remember the smells of the cattails' smoldering.

March 3 —
Redwing blackbird
laying claim to his
spring territory
in the marsh.
He's calling from
a leftover cattail
of last year — all
downy and still
blowing on the wind.
Redwings and cattails —
the early spring marsh —
I can almost smell
it coming to
life.

AUGUST 12, Goldenrod

August has the reputation of being hot and sultry, but there are cool nights that give us a temporary relief and hint of the approach of autumn. To be sure there are other signs that fall is fast approaching; the first migrating birds are beginning to appear; the northern water thrushes are pausing by slow-moving streams on their southward flight; tree swallows are gathering in flocks; cranberries and blackberries are beginning to deepen in color; the curved stems of the Solomon's seal are heavy with blackish berries; the currentlike clusters of the chokecherries are hanging in thickets; the scarlet berries of the nightshade shine like red lanterns in shady tangles; and the goldenrods are beginning to dress the fields in a cloth of gold.

The goldenrods are perennial herbs mostly with wandlike stems, sessile or nearly sessile alternate, usually toothed leaves, yellow disk and ray flowers (except for one species) in small heads, each surrounded by an involucre consisting of a few or more appressed scales (bracts), heads very numerous and crowded in sometimes one-sided clusters, or these branched and consisting of compound panicles or racemes, the fruit an achene.

The goldenrods are so common and such a familiar feature of the late summer and autumn landscape that we take them for granted. I detached a flowering stem once and examined it with a magnifying glass and was surprised at what I saw—a row of tiny yellow goblets. Each goblet, of course, is a flower head.

There are some 140 species of goldenrods, most of which occur in the New World, a few in Europe and Asia. Unless one is a trained botanist, it would be futile to try to identify any but those that have some rather obvious and distinguishing characteristic. Some of the more easily recognizable of the common species are the following: *blue-stemmed goldenrod*, a late-blooming graceful, dainty species found along shady roadsides and in moist woods and thickets; *broad-leaved* or *zigzag goldenrod*, of woodlands and thicket borders with brilliant, beautiful yellow flowers and a stem that grows as if it were not quite sure which direction to take; *bog goldenrod*, of swamps and bogs, a densely flowered species; *early goldenrod*, of dry rocky banks and roadsides, perhaps the first of our goldenrods to blossom, easily recognized by the peculiarity of its recurved stems and whose usually beautiful branching panicles are so often dried for winter decoration; *rough-stemmed goldenrod*, an exceedingly hairy species and very common on wooded roadsides, sometimes with a stem only a foot high, at other times as much as seven feet; *gray goldenrod*, remarkable for its rich, deep golden yellow flowers and its simple unbranched gray green stem that, with the

April 16 —
Took a walk today — a nice spring day and needed a little time off and sunshine. It amazes me as I cross the field how so many of last year's weed and flower stalks are still standing and recognizable. Goldenrod, so fine and delicate, has survived the ice, snow, and winter winds buffeting it. Without its flowers, I can see its simple structure clearly.

leaves, is covered with minute grayish hairs and found along sandy roads and in dry pastures; *white goldenrod* or *silverrod*, the only species with white flowers; *Canada goldenrod*, undoubtedly the most beautiful of all our goldenrods, with its spreading densely flowered panicle with recurved sprays that crowns a stem often as much as eight feet high; and *sweet goldenrod*, a goldenrod of thicket borders, open woodlands, and sunny hillsides that appeals to both our sight and smell. The leaves of sweet goldenrod when crushed give off a pleasant anise scent. This is the only goldenrod I know of that has been found to be of some use; the leaves when dried and steeped in water produce a pleasant beverage, said to be a good substitute for tea. Hence this goldenrod is also known as Blue Mountain Tea.

It has often been said that no flower attracts as many insects as the goldenrod. I don't know how true this is, but countless insects do visit the flowers. Among the more frequent visitors are the honeybee, bumblebee, mining and carpenter bee, chalcid fly, soldier beetle, the locust borer (a beautiful black beetle with numerous wavy yellow bands), and the blister beetle (a black beetle frequently found in such numbers that the golden plumes appear to be sprinkled with soot).

In view of their abundance and availability it is somewhat surprising that the use by wildlife of the goldenrods is low. True, some gamebirds do feed on the leaves, some songbirds on the seeds, and some mammals on both, but to a very limited extent. Even so, along our roadside, they are a welcome signal of a new season to come. For that, I like them.

September 30—

Hundreds of monarch butterflies gather on the goldenrod during their migration— several groups of them along a coastal road. The monarchs are making their way south to their wintering grounds.

What a sight— the goldenrod is sagging.

AUGUST 17, Aster

One of the glories of late summer and early fall is the multitude of asters that blossom along the roadsides and in woodland thickets, in field and meadow, and on the distant hillsides. Asters bloom in tones of blue, violet, purple, and white. Of course the asters begin to flower in midsummer, but it is in the fall that they seem to come into their own and we begin to appreciate their distinctive beauty. Their colors are not vivid and dazzling, yet they are warm and harmonious with a sort of subdued glow that is both arresting and appealing to my eye.

The asters were not always so appealing. At some time long ago, the flowers were probably only simple green leaves that surrounded the reproductive organs. Like the grasses, they may have depended on the wind to transfer their pollen. Then subtle changes began to take place and continued to occur for a long time; the outer row of stamens gradually was changed into colorful petals that caught the eye of insects, and tubular flowers were evolved that secreted nectar that appealed to their taste. The stamens then became attached to the inside walls of the tubes so that their pollen could cover the insects as they crawled over them. Finally great numbers of tubular flowers became massed together so that they could readily be found by the insects. And the insects, too, underwent subtle changes, as if they and the plants both knew and appreciated each other's requirements and tried to become mutually compatible.

There are some 250 species of asters; few botanists know them all. Though they are easy to recognize as asters, many are difficult to identify as species, even by trained observers. But for most of us, it is enough to contemplate their beauty as we wander about the countryside. And yet there are some so distinctive that we can recognize them at a glance—as for instance, the heath aster (also known as the Michaelmas daisy), a bushy plant of fields, roadsides, and waste places with masses of small white flowers with yellow disks that look like miniature daisies. The asters, so rich in nectar, are an autumnal favorite of the honeybee.

September 18 —
   Asters — the flowers of
the fall. I can't pass
them by out in the field without
stopping to pick
some and then
adding Queen
Anne's lace to
bring inside —
the ivory lace
and violet
asters are
beautiful
together.

↑ Late purple aster
very violet blue.

AUGUST 23, Caterpillar

Consider the caterpillar. If one watches carefully, it can be seen that this creature moves with grace and dignity.

Destructive? It is merely a matter of perspective. And aren't humans destructive? Probably far more so, as humanity gradually is destroying its environment and some day may not have a place to live. That cannot be said of caterpillars, since nature sees to it that the caterpillars and their environment are kept in balance.

Ugly? Far from it. Many caterpillars are quite attractive. And a few are really beautiful, such as the white-marked tussock moth with its coral-red head, three long pencils of black hairs, and four white tussocks.

The caterpillar with which most budding naturalists are familiar is the woolly bear, the evenly clipped, black-and-red hairy caterpillar that in late summer moves over the ground in apparent haste. The amount of black in the woolly bear's "fur" varies greatly and is supposed to foretell the coming winter weather. I suspect it is a record of past weather rather than of the future, as the amount of black is determined by the wetness or dryness of the animal's environment. Moist conditions promote a greater amount of black, and dry conditions induce a preponderance of red.

There are other "bears" such as the yellow bear that I find frequently in our garden. Its name is somewhat misleading since its long dense hairs may be white or reddish. More consistent in appearance is the harlequin caterpillar. It is very black with tufts of yellow hairs along the back, a most striking little creature. Sometimes we find in our garden a fourth kind of hairy caterpillar; this one's long hairs are sometimes black and sometimes brown, and of a lighter brown on the sides. Its most inappropriate name is the salt-marsh caterpillar. To be sure it may be found in marshes along the coast, but being a general feeder it may occur almost anywhere. Which calls to mind that the hickory tiger, a snow-white, black-dotted, black-tufted caterpillar, is found not only on hickory but also on other trees as well.

In all these caterpillars the hairs grow in spreading clusters from warts, a condition that should lead us to suspect that they are all members of the same family as, indeed, they are. And they all transform into small moths known as the tiger moths. Some of these moths are exceedingly pretty.

At about the same time that we see the woolly bear we may see also the yellow, hairy American dagger caterpillar crawling along a city sidewalk, also in search of a snug retreat in which to curl up for the winter. Hairs are a sort of clothing and function primarily as protection because

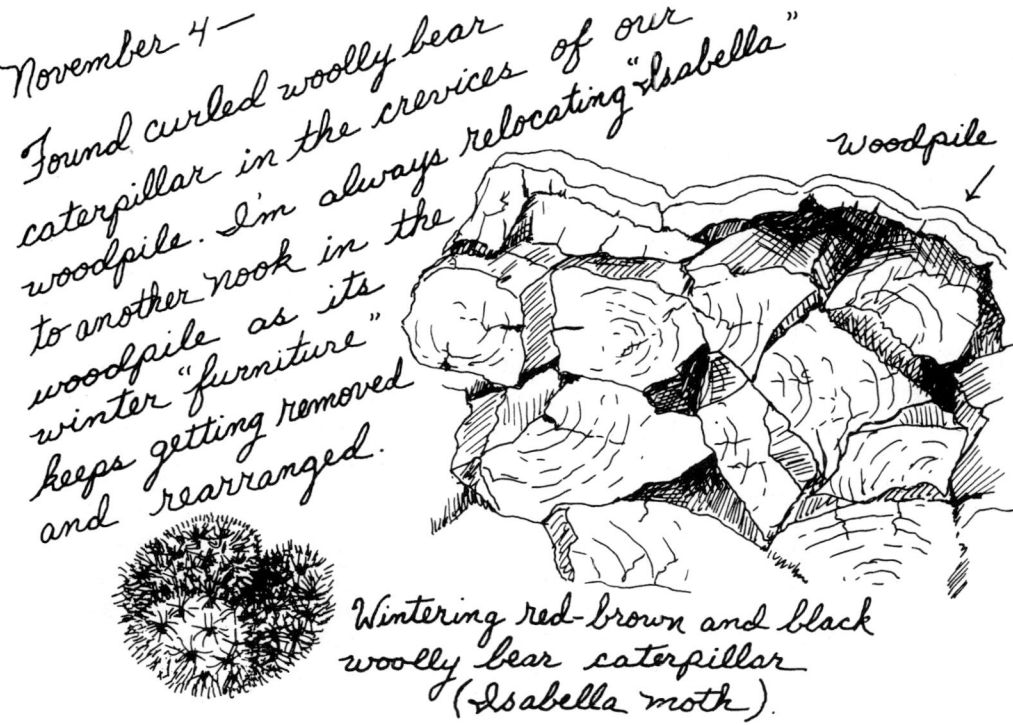

November 4 —
Found curled woolly bear caterpillar in the crevices of our woodpile. I'm always relocating "Isabella" to another nook in the woodpile as its winter "furniture" keeps getting removed and rearranged.

Wintering red-brown and black woolly bear caterpillar (Isabella moth).

woodpile

birds generally leave hairy caterpillars alone. They also are effective in protecting some hibernating caterpillars, such as the woolly bears, from sudden changes in temperature.

In some caterpillars the hairs are associated with glands; they serve as an outlet for secretions that frequently are poisonous, as in the case of the caterpillars of the brown-tail moth. These caterpillars are clothed with white and brown hairs. The brown hairs are barbed and emit a fluid that produces a skin inflammation similar to that produced by poison ivy and known as brown-tail rash. Indeed, we can acquire the rash without handling the caterpillars; at the time of molting the hairs are freed and are carrier by the wind, sometimes gaining entrance to our skin without our being aware of it, until the inflammation sets in.

Other caterpillars are armed with venomous spines, as that of the io moth, which everyone should learn to recognize. The caterpillar is green with a broad brown or reddish stripe on each side of the abdomen, edged below with white; the spines, tipped with black, are not only sharp but also brittle and easily broken. Venomous spines also occur on the saddleback caterpillar, the spiny oak slug, and the hag moth caterpillar. The saddleback caterpillar can be recognized by its curious shape and the large green patch that resembles a saddle cloth, the saddle itself being represented by an oval purplish-brown spot. The spiny oak slug is oval in shape, greenish, and variably marked with red and pale-orange stripes. The hag moth caterpillar has a number of plumelike or hairy appendages that have a backward twist like a lock of disheveled hair, reminding one of an old hag, hence its name. All three caterpillars are sluglike in appearance with almost nothing resembling legs.

Some caterpillars, like those of the swallowtail butterflies, when disturbed give off a liquid with an indescribably repellent odor. Caterpillars of butterflies generally known as the blues secrete a substance called honeydew; this substance attracts ants that presumably protect the caterpillars.

A few caterpillars obtain protection through their acrid taste derived from the food they eat. A different type of defense is presented by the familiar milkweed caterpillar. This caterpillar has a pair of threadlike black "horns" on top of the second segment and a short pair on the eleventh. When the caterpillar becomes frightened or disturbed the front "horns" twist excitedly; they presumably keep away parasitic flies that otherwise would lay their eggs on the caterpillar. Other caterpillars wear color or color patters that blend with their background, thus escaping detection or are so vividly colored or have such hideous markings that these presumably frighten away potential attackers, the caterpillar of the tiger swallowtail being a case in point. Finally there is the hickory horned devil, our largest caterpillar. It is a ferocious-looking creature with its long, spiny, reddish horns tipped with black, but it is perfectly harmless.

The amateur entomologist may not know the tent caterpillar as an individual, but he or she is probably acquainted with the large silken tents the insect spins in spring among the tree branches. Examine one of these tents or webs and one will find it occupied by numerous velvety-black, hairy, caterpillars that remain together until full-grown. They rest in the web during storms and during the heat of the day, emerging to feed when it is cooler. They seem to follow definite paths, which can be recognized by the silken threads they spin as they pass along branches or the stems of leaves, feeding.

In September as in April, one may see large silken tents or webs on various trees and many persons suppose the fall tents to be the same that they saw in the spring. But these second tents are made by an entirely different insect, the fall webworm. In both cases the tent is at first small, but as the caterpillars feed and grow the tent becomes larger and soiled by the excrement, the molted skins, and bits of leaf clippings tht become incorporated in the silk. Fall webworms are yellowish and variably marked with black and brown, with such great variations in markings that you may examine hundreds and not find two exactly alike.

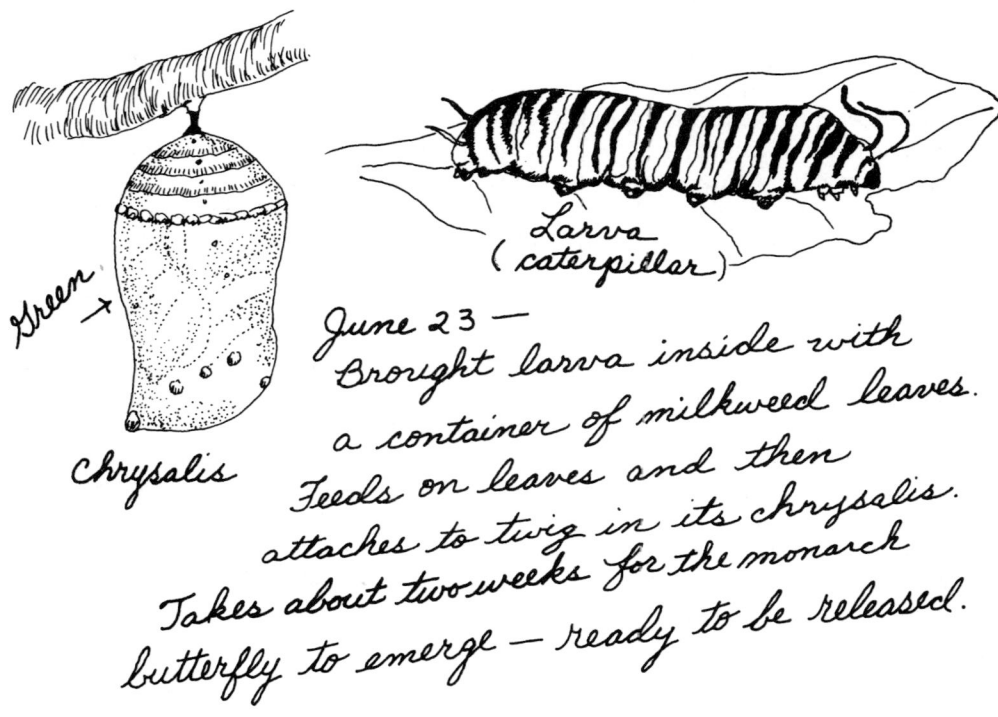

Less conspicuous is the communal web made by the caterpillars of the Baltimore butterfly, in which they feed gregariously until autumn when they hibernate in it. Tent caterpillars and the fall webworm, on the other hand, spend the winter in cocoons.

A silken tent or web is not essential to communal feeding, as other caterpillars feed gregariously without such a protective covering. I have in mind the red-humped apple worm, which I have recently found feeding on a nearby wild blackberry, although it is more common on the apple. They crowd so close together that they cover a branch completely. And I still can recall the time I found a willow so densely populated by the caterpillars of the mourning cloak butterfly that the leaves—or what was left of them—were barely visible.

Although some caterpillars, such as the milkweed caterpillar, are restricted to one or two food plants, and others to members of a single plant family, many range over a great number of different plants. The caterpillar of the cecropia moth feeds on more than sixty species representing thirty-one genera, and the yellow bear, which we have mentioned, feeds indifferently on all kinds of herbage. But the gypsy moth "holds the record"—its caterpillar will eat almost any plant, more than five hundred different species being included in its diet.

Most grownups fondly remember the measuring worms or inch worms that fascinate children by their gait. They are quite common on trees and shrubs but often escape detection by clinging to a twig with their hind legs (prolegs) and extending their bodies outward so that they look very much like a twig. They can remain in such a position indefinitely by spinning a silk thread or guy rope from their mouths and attaching it to the twig.

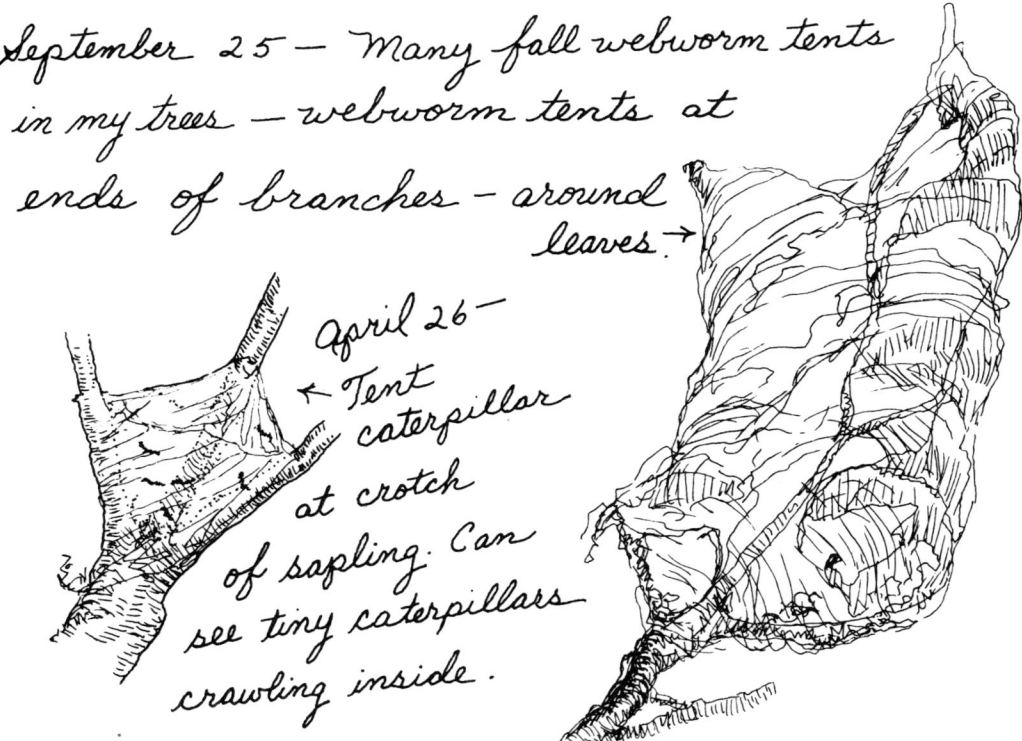

September 25 — Many fall webworm tents in my trees — webworm tents at ends of branches — around leaves. →

April 26 — ← Tent caterpillar at crotch of sapling. Can see tiny caterpillars crawling inside.

AUGUST 28, Crayfish

Although most gourmets have heard of the crayfish (a.k.a. crawfish or "crawdads"), few have seen the living animal, a common inhabitant of ponds and streams. I saw my first crayfish one summer many years ago when, as a boy, I was exploring a brook and suddenly saw a dark object moving along the bottom. Heedless of what the consequences might be I plunged my hand into the water and grabbed the moving object; holding it aloft I recognized it as a crayfish. Examining it carefully so that every feature would be indelibly impressed on my mind, I finally dropped it in the water and saw it scurry away.

The crayfish is an edible relative of the lobster, crab, and shrimp. With the exception of the southern freshwater prawns it is the only freshwater representative of the group of animals known as the decapods (named from their ten legs).

The crayfish looks and behaves much like the lobster, differing only in size and minor details. Its distinguishing feature is its first pair of legs, each of which is provided with a conspicuous and formidable nipper or pincer, that serve as both offensive and defensive weapons.

There are a number of species of crayfish. Some live in lakes and some in both slow and swift streams; others prefer muddy ponds and ditches and burrow into the banks if the ponds and ditches dry up; and still others burrow in wet meadows, never actually going into the water. The species that live in water are rarely found in water over five feet deep.

Crayfish burrows vary in size and in complexity of structure, and range in depth from a few inches to eight or ten feet, depending on the water level. The terminal chamber in which the crayfish spends the day must be wet. The excavated soil is usually piled up around the entrance, occasionally forming "chimneys" that may be of considerable height; some species of crayfish excavate burrows that extend below the frost line and down to the ground water. In winter and summer when lakes and streams recede, such burrowers enter their tunnels, plug up the opening, and retire to their underground cisterns of ground water where they remain in a more or less inactive state. In winter crayfish are sluggish and lethargic, move slowly about, and increase in size very little or not at all and thus do not molt.

The crayfish is essentially nocturnal in habit, although on cloudy days and in shady streams we may often see it crawling about on the bottom by day. For the most part it rests or hides beneath a stone or in its burrow where it lies in wait for a fish or water insect, which it captures and tears to pieces with its big pincers. It also lives on living plants as well as on

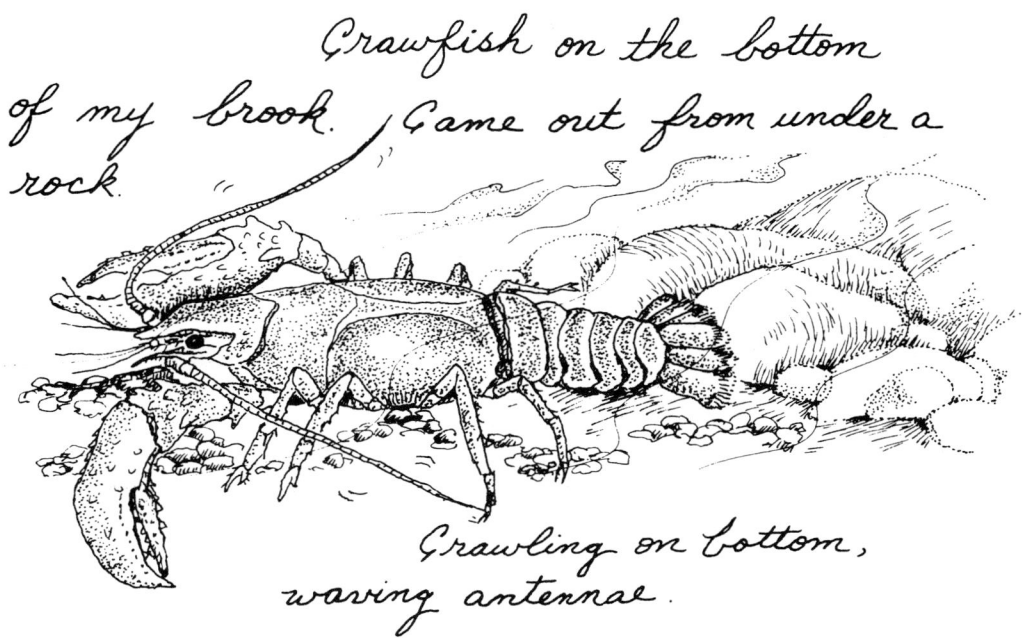

Crawfish on the bottom of my brook. Came out from under a rock.

Crawling on bottom, waving antennae.

decaying plant and animal substances. In turn it falls prey to fishes, wading birds, frogs, turtles, and such mammals as the raccoon, otter, and mink—and I suppose we should add man. The animal is able to move forward, backward, and sideways with equal facility, its movements being as a rule rather slow. When frightened or alarmed it will swim quickly backwards, with vigorous downward strokes of its abdomen.

Some species of crayfish appear translucent; others are heavily pigmented with black, brown red, orange red, or blue, frequently with mottling. At times they may exhibit a great deal of color variation, one species ranging through all the colors mentioned above. Quite frequently the color or shade is determined by the nature of the background, the result of the chromatophores (the light-sensitive color cells) being able to open and close and thus expose varying amounts of the pigment granules that they contain.

Some species of crayfish mate in the fall and spawn in the spring; others mate throughout the year. It appears that the males are unable to distinguish between the sexes during the breeding season because they try to mate with any crayfish they encounter. At the time of mating the sperms are transferred to the seminal receptacles (saclike organs that receive and

A story on the edge of the brook. A raccoon visited here and left its footprints — also left evidence that it had eaten a crayfish. I can picture the raccoon fishing around with his paws, patting and investigating all the crevices and overturning the rocks until his "fingers" grasp his dinner.

store sperms) of the female, and when the eggs are laid several weeks or several months later they are then fertilized. The eggs are not deposited in the water but are attached to the swimmerets (abdominal appendages that function as swimming organs) by means of a sticky substance and are aerated by being moved back and forth in the water. They hatch in two months or so and the young crayfish, which have the form of their parents, attach themselves to the swimmerets and are carried about until they can shift for themselves.

The crayfish makes a novel and hardy aquarium pet and can be kept for a long time if some simple precautions are followed. The aquarium should be supplied with a little mud, some water plants, and a stone or flat rock that rises slightly above the water line. The water should not be permitted to become polluted and should be changed as often as necessary. Sudden temperature changes should be avoided; it should not be allowed to rise above sixty-five degrees Fahrenheit. Crayfish may be fed bits of raw meat, chopped raw fish, earthworms, and water insects, but they should not be fed to the full demand of their appetites as they will then become inert and sluggish.

The crayfish seem to have the ability to learn by experience; I have been able to train them to come to take their food from a pair of forceps.

SEPTEMBER 1, Cricket

Cowper wrote of the cricket at the hearth, and his lines can well be applied to our own common field cricket, whose tune, though not quite so cheerful perhaps, is nonetheless pleasing, especially when heard in the quiet of a summer's evening. I have often lain awake on a summer night listening to their serenades or concerts when they play together until drowsiness gradually steals over me and I finally fall asleep.

Although one may hear a lone cricket playing its fiddle in early spring, it is not until summer has arrived that countless crickets begin to tune their instruments and throughout the night fill the air with their orchestral music. And yet, though we may be conscious of their playing it is not until summer is almost gone and September is upon us that we seem to take more notice of their concerts. Is it because the birds have become noticeably silent and the cicadas have ceased their monotonous buzzing? Is it because other instrumentalists have put aside their music making for another year, leaving the crickets in sole possession of their human audience?

Almost everyone is acquainted with the field cricket and its patent-leather finish. It is commonly found in grassy pasture land or fields, where it lives in a burrow under the ground or merely beneath a board or stone. It is for the most part nocturnal and solitary in habits, concealing itself by day and coming out from its retreat to seek its food at night. The eggs of the field cricket are laid singly in holes in the ground, which the females make with their sharp-pointed ovipositors, and hatch the following summer.

How does a cricket chirp? First, only the males chirp. They may be distinguished from the females by the absence of an ovipositor, a long swordlike structure that extends backwards from the tip of the female's abdomen. Second, one will observe that the male raises its wing covers to an angle of forty-five degrees and rubs them together. Actually there is more to it than this, for if one examines one of the wing covers closely, as with a magnifying glass or hand lens, it can be seen that the veins form a peculiar scroll pattern that serves as a framework for making a sounding board of the wing membrane by stretching it out like a drumhead.

Near the base of the wing there is a heavy crossvein covered with transverse ridges, called a file, and on the inner side of the same wing near the base, a hardened area known as the scraper. The cricket sounds its note by drawing the scraper of the underwing cover against the file of the overlapping one. We can produce a similar sound by running a file along the edge of a tin can.

As the wing covers are excellent sounding boards (tympani) and

*August 24 —
Crickets calling —
summer nights
windows open,
night air warm —
crickets calling —
smell sweet hay —
third cutting —
and still
the crickets call.*

*Differences
male field cricket*

Female field cricket

← *Ovipositor*

quiver when the notes are made, they set the surrounding air to vibrating, thus giving rise to sound waves that travel a considerable distance. It is interesting to note that the cricket can use its wings alternately—that is, use one wing cover as a scraper and the other as a file and then reverse them, thus reducing their wear and tear.

At one time it was believed that male crickets chirp to attract females, but this view was discarded when it was found that the females do not always respond to their chirps. Actually, their chirps, as we hear them, have no meaning to the crickets. We now know that when crickets chirp, they also produce notes too highly pitched to be audible to us. It is these ultrasonic notes that they use to communicate with one another, the chirps being merely incidental. It has also been established that the field cricket has at least three basic sound signals: a calling note, an aggressive chirp, and a curious song. On the tibia of each front leg is a small white disklike spot; it is the auditory organ or ear.

Crickets make interesting pets and are most companionable, especially on winter nights when they evoke memories of the summer with their chirping. They can be kept in a goldfish bowl or in a wire cage containing a little soil and may be fed lettuce, moist bread, and various fruits. If the zookeeper in the family attempts to keep a large family of crickets, it would be best to give them some bonemeal to prevent them from eating each other.

SEPTEMBER 8, Fringed Gentian

Although the asters and goldenrods appear to be the dominant wildflowers of the autumn landscape, many others are still in bloom: The daisy fleabane flowers are in fields and along roadsides everywhere; the Jerusalem artichoke's bright yellow flowers gleam like miniature suns above the fence rows; and the blazing star decorates waste places with its soft rose-purple flower heads. One can still find ladies' tresses in wet meadows, where also patches of lavender pink gerardia peep above the grasses; the bur marigolds shimmer along the fringes of ponds and streams, and the chickweed and shepherd's purse never seem to stop flowering.

All these flowers are rather commonplace, and we take them more or less for granted. But not so the fringed gentian, becoming so rare that it is a happy occasion when we chance upon it. I have never forgotten the day when I came upon this gay and lovely flower for the first time, in a shady patch that fringed a woodland pool; it was a memorable event when I recorded it in my notebook.

The fringed gentian, which naively lavishes its blandishments upon the moist situations it has decided to honor, is remarkable for the delicate misty quality of its blue color and the expressiveness of its flower form, which is deep vase-shaped with four rounded, light lavender-blue lobes deeply fringed and spreading horizontally in the sunshine. Thoreau likened its color to that of the male bluebird. The fringed gentian is a late-blooming flower, as William Cullen Bryant wrote in his "To the Fringed Gentian."

It is always a delight to find the gentian in blossom, which is not often. It is becoming much too rare because many people cannot resist picking it. In the autumn, the little seeds germinate when and where they find soft, moist soil. As the plant is a biennial its seeds *alone* perpetuate it. The fringed gentian may not reappear in the same places year after year; we do not know when or where we will next find it. Even though we may revisit the spot the following year, we may search for it in vain.

October 6 — In a field, near road, a nice group of blue fringed gentian — beautiful color growing near a small country town.

Have also seen closed gentian in forest in late summer —

← Deeper blue

Violet ← blue

SEPTEMBER 26, Sumac

As the cool nights of declining summer herald the approach of autumn, the red maples are beginning to unfurl their scarlet flags to advertize the great annual show that autumn stages before ringing down the final curtain on the dying year. Now the glories of the sunrise are repeated in the sunset glow, and during the day the landscape is painted with colors that rival those of spring. Much of the brilliance of the autumn landscape is due to the red maples, whose scarlet or crimson leaves stand out against the azure sky. But they are not alone, for the red oak now becomes clothed in a rich, dark-purplish red, the scarlet oak stands aglow with fire, and on the uplands the beech appears with leaves of palest Naples yellow, while the gray birch adds a touch of beauty to rocky barrens, old fields, and waste places with brilliant golden leaves that glisten beneath dancing sunbeams. And what would the radiant splendor of the autumn foliage be without the gorgeous coloring of the sugar maple?

But the sumacs are no less wonderful and contribute their share to the pageant. They glow in scarlet and gold, often deepening to crimson and orange, and fling their magnificent beauty along fences, over deserted fields, and up rocky, gravelly mountainsides.

Most tree watchers are acquainted with the staghorn sumac (so named because of the resemblance of its rich velvety, thick, leafless twigs to the new antlers of the stag). Personally I think we are more conscious of its presence in winter, when we see its antlered branches held aloft like candelabra, its pointed red fruit clusters silhouetted against the snow-covered landscape like flaming torches.

In winter this tree—or shrub if you prefer, for it is not always a tree—stands naked, its architecture is revealed as being rather unshapely, somewhat stiff, awkward, and clumsy. In summer, in full panoply of foliage, the tree acquires an entirely different, almost beautiful, character with its fernlike leaves that lift and sway with every passing breeze. Among the leaves appear the whitish-green or yellow-green flowers in dense, conical hairy clusters, with the staminate and pistillate on separate trees. The pistillate flowers develop into tiny, globular acid drupes that are covered with deep-red hairs and are clustered in large, compact panicles that remain on the tree during the winter and provide a festive board for birds as well as other forms of wildlife. (This fruit is sour, but this sourness once served a useful purpose. If the drupes—or "berries," as they are sometimes called—are placed in water for a short time, they make a pleasing and agreeable drink known as "Indian lemonade.")

April 18 —
Sumac seed heads are still providing for the wildlife. Some are thinned out and very sparse. Others completely gone of berries from winter and feeding.

The other day a mockingbird stopped to feed in the sumac berries. A robin visits next.

← Furry stem like "a deer's antlers in velvet."

Chickadees and a score of others live on sumac.

Staghorn sumac shape →

There are some 120 species of sumacs, 16 being found in North America, only a few of which are actual trees. They form the temperate-zone genus of a great tropical family (*Cashew*) that contains some 400 species, which are widely distributed throughout Africa, Asia, North and South America, the Indian Archipelago, Australia, and the Sandwich Islands. As for the name sumac—which has been variously spelled *sumach, shumac, summaque,* and *shumack*—it is said to have been derived from the Arabic name for a species occurring in the Mediterranean, *si.nmak* or *summaq*. Sumac by any name, I enjoy its September color.

AUTUMN

September 22 —

The air has that "fallen leaves" smell. Backyard birds pulling out after spending the summer raising their families. Hawk migration in full swing — can watch the ridge and Sunrise Mountain from the yard. Many broadwing hawks fill the sky, riding the thermals south.

Among the most memorable recollections that I have cherished through the years as a naturalist are those associated with the birds that nested in my garden and outside my study where I could observe their activities at close range and the countless patrons of my avian "restaurants" who seemed to like what I had to offer.

The kinds of birds that might visit, either as temporary guests or more or less permanent residents, depend, of course, on where one lives. In Massachusetts, for instance, we might expect to have for temporary guests in winter the black-capped chickadee, white-breasted nuthatch, goldfinch, tree sparrow, and junco. In the spring we could expect the bluebird, robin, catbird, house wren; they would come seeking nesting sites and perhaps materials with which to build their nests.

There have been years when the catbirds nested in a clump of lilacs that grew near a corner of my house and on such occasions I would again have the opportunity to observe their strange courtship rituals. The robin, too, has often nested near my house. There was one year when a robin family selected a cedar that was directly outside our dining room window, and from that vantage point I was able to follow their daily activities: the building of the nest (by the female), the incubation of the eggs, and the rearing of the young until such time as they were able to leave the nest. (One disadvantage of this site was that the robin often saw his reflection in the window and would then attack it; this intermittent thumping against the glass continued for weeks.)

Though many of us recognize the robin, few actually know much about it. For instance, the robin is not a robin at all—never has been, and never will be. The real robin is a native of the Old World, a small bird formed somewhat like our bluebird with a dark-brown back and a reddish-orange throat and breast. It is the bird we so often find in European literature and folklore, the one that covered the "Babes in the Wood" with leaves. There is also a Breton legend that attributes the bird's red breast to injuries sustained while plucking the thorns from our Saviour's crown on the cross. The American robin is a rather large bird with a reddish brown or tawny breast and was so named by the early English colonists in memory of their own robin. Despite attempts to change the bird's name, we still know it as the robin and probably always will.

Many birders also don't realize that many of the robins seen in northern states throughout the warm months of the year remain during the winter as well, roosting in the evergreen swamps, feeding on winter berries and other fruits, and sometimes appearing in a field during a thaw when the snow has disappeared. Most of the robins, however, do go south in the fall, to return the following spring.

During the winter months in South Carolina both the white-crowned and white-throated sparrows are temporary guests quite frequently visit-

May 8 — a house wren is scolding me from the side of the beaver pond — where the maidenhair ferns grow.

ing the cafeteria outside my dining-room window. Both species are winter residents, but their visits are somewhat sporadic; they will appear daily for several days at a time, then there will be a hiatus of another few days, then suddenly they will reappear.

The tufted titmouse is also an erratic guest despite the fact that it lives in South Carolina throughout the year. It is a delightful little bird, in habits much like the chickadee. It has a great deal of curiosity and easily becomes quite tame and confiding. There are days in succession when I will see the titmouse at the "cafeteria," and then it will disappear again for several weeks.

Other birds such as the redwing, grackle, cowbird, starling, and rusty blackbird are infrequent visitors, but since they do not tarry long I do not consider them guests—rather, curiosity seekers. And invariably each year, usually sometime in January, a flock of cedar waxwings, those Beau Brummells of birdland, will suddenly appear from nowhere and descend upon my holly trees, to strip them of their berries in a matter of minutes, then to disappear as suddenly and as quickly as they appeared. I do not regard the waxwings as guests either, more as thieves; though I don't begrudge them the berries they eat. If it were not for the mess they leave behind I would be more inclined to be amused by their behavior, for they feed like gluttons.

And, as in Massachusetts, in some years a pair of catbirds will appropriate a mock-orange shrub and remain near the house until they have raised their family, when they will take off for parts unknown. I always welcome the catbirds, for they are amusing birds. Some are indifferent singers, but others are highly gifted. At times the male will sing his carol almost continuously for hours, and especially when his mate is confined to her nest he will sing, as one writer put it, in an "ecstasy of delight."

Some people I know resent having the mockingbird around the house because of its habit of singing quite early in the morning or at night—by the light of the moon—and thus disturbing human sleep. But it is merely a matter of getting used to it, as I found out, when it ceases to be disturbing.

The mockingbird in recent years has been extending its range and now occurs in New England; but when I lived there it was seen only upon a rare occasion. It was not until I moved to South Carolina that I was really able to become acquainted with the mockingbird and to learn to appreciate its marvelous repertoire of songs, perhaps the most extensive of any of our songsters. I also discovered what a mimic this bird is, though I was aware of its talents in this direction. And as I see its flashing white in the sunlight as it takes to wing, the buoyancy of the mockingbird's actions appeals to the eye no less than its music captivates the ear.

The mockingbirds are permanent residents in my yard. Each year they build their nest in one of the bushes, or rather the female does, though the male assists her from time to time. But before the actual building takes place they engage in a unique courtship performance that is well worth observing.

The mockingbird male is a rather pugnacious bird—especially during the nesting period—and I have often seen him attack the larger blue jay as the latter appears at one of my "cafeterias." The blue jay is more or less a permanent guest, though his visits are somewhat erratic. What few people know is that the blue jay is second only to the mockingbird as an imitator, though most of its imitations are apparently not presented near human ears.

It would seem that everyone in the South, where the cardinal is a familiar bird, would know it by name. Yet there are some southern folk who refer to it merely as "the red bird," a name perhaps more appropriately applied to the male summer tanager, which is completely red, whereas the cardinal has a black face and a black patch at the base of its bill.

The cardinal near my home is a permanent guest, and hardly a day passes that I don't see him or his mate about the house or at one of the feeding stations. The cardinal is one of those rare songsters that will sing in every month of the year, his song being a series of loud but melodious whistles, one of the common notes being very much like a whistle used in calling a dog; as a matter of fact, dogs are often deceived by it.

Although I have often seen the towhee in New England, I can't recall it ever appearing in my own yard or garden there. But here in South Carolina it seems to have taken more or less permanent possession of my yard; I see it every day at my feeding stations or running over the ground looking for seeds of insects among the fallen leaves. The towhee is a ground bird, being rarely seen high in a tree, and a rather noisy bird, as it rustles the leaves on the ground or scratches like a fox sparrow with both feet; even in flight its wing strokes are noisy.

Although the brown thrasher is normally a bird of thickets, bushy pastures, and brier patches, a pair of these birds became bold enough last year to appear in my yard; they nested in the tangled vines lining the stone wall that separates my grounds from my neighbors'. They are shy birds. At my appearance they quickly sought the safety of the bushy undergrowth. Most of their time they spend on the ground seeking insects among the fallen leaves, and hence they are welcome visitors, eaters of obnoxious pests. But insects form only part of their diet, which includes fruits, acorns, and the like when they become available. As I write this, they are absent, having disappeared sometime during the fall, and I am curious to see if they return in the spring.

January 7 — Male rufus-sided towhee has remained here through the winter, feeding on the bird feeder tray (4 feet above the ground) as well as on the ground.

← Black

Perched on this icy cold day among the bittersweet vines. So many of the birds prefer the shelter of these vines.

March 23 —

Rainy and cool — phoebe (one neighbors with me every year) is calling his phoebe song from the highest spire of a spruce tree — declaring his rights and possessions — and seeking his mate. I usually see phoebe much closer to the ground — you look out of place way up there, phoebe.

OCTOBER 1, Spider

To see a rather unusual sight, I can go outdoors into the nearest field or even my own backyard on a soft October day when the sun shines brightly and a gentle breeze flows over the landscape. I will see countless miniature parachutes sailing through the air, each presumably carrying a milkweed, dandelion, thistle seed, or some other seed similarly equipped. But if one looks closely at some of these silken parachutes, it will be discovered that they are carrying small spiders instead of seeds.

The aviation and aerospace industries take considerable pride in what we have accomplished in navigating through the air, but spiders have been doing it for a long, long time, perhaps from the time they first appeared on the earth. When a spider feels the urge to go ballooning, it climbs to the summit of the nearest promontory, which may be a plant, a spike of grass, a fence post or fence rail, and faces the direction of the wind. Then it extends its eight legs, four on each side, secures a firm purchase on its support, and then elevates its abdomen to an angle of about forty-five degrees so that its body is raised above its perch. At the tip of the abdomen are the spinnerets, fingerlike appendages covered with minute spinning spools, through which jets of silk are forced from a multitude of glands within the body. The liquid silk hardens on contact with the air in the form of threads that are seized and drawn out by the air currents to a length of, sometimes, as much as twenty feet.

These threads are held apart or combined at the spider's will by the closing or the outspreading of the spinnerets. Meanwhile, as the threads are carried out by the air currents, the spider's legs incline toward the breeze and the joints stiffen, the entire attitude of the spider showing the muscular strain it is undergoing in resisting an uplifting force.

The spider continues the spinning process until it instinctively knows that this uplifting force is sufficient to support it in the air, then it disengages its feet from its perch and takes off, to float in the air in whichever direction the air currents carry it.

The spider is not, however, completely at the mercy of the air currents, as one might suppose, but is able to exercise a certain amount of control over its "balloon" by climbing about the silken threads and by pulling in and winding up the silken filaments or by spinning more of them.

At one time it was believed that the aeronautic habit was the monopoly of a single species or was limited to a certain time of the year. But it is now known that it is not the exclusive right of a single species; ballooning can be indulged in at almost any time, though it most frequently occurs in the spring and fall when immense numbers of young spiders emerge from

June 1 — Watching a male yellow-rumped warbler (myrtle warbler) flitting around me — seems to be seeking out a meal among the branches. A spider. I can see the spider's thread, and warbler can see the spider!

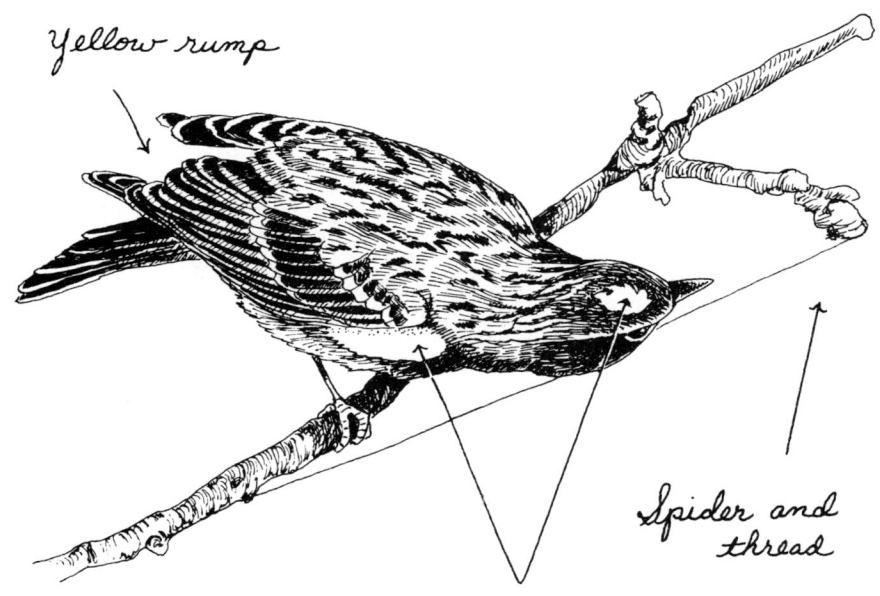

Yellow rump

Spider and thread

Yellow on head and sides of breast.

the egg sacs. It is at such times that they attract our attention by their large numbers.

Small spiders may often be made to take off by blowing steadily against them, and sometimes very tiny spiders, weighing very little, are suddenly wafted into the air when they least expect it. Even the larger spiders when dropping on their draglines are frequently caught by the wind and blown no inconsiderable distance.

The ballooning goes on at heights up to 200 feet but powerful air currents often carry the small aeronauts up to as high as 10,000 feet. The object of the spiders' wind-blown flights is presumed to be the dispersal of the species and doubtless is effective. That the ballooning spiders are often carried considerable distances is shown by the fact that they have been picked up by ships at sea several hundred miles from land.

Sometimes spiders attempt to balloon when the wind is too strong. Then the threads that they have spun are not lifted up but instead are blown against some object; and thus large fields are often covered with a gauze of silk. At other times sheets of silk are formed by the massing together of numberless strands in such situations that the sheets are finally torn away by the wind and later deposited elsewhere, producing the showers of gossamer celebrated in prose and poetry.

July 17 —
The golden garden spider has made its orb web just outside the kitchen window in my garden — easy to watch. On the inside of the window my resident house spiders — which seem to occupy every corner of the house — do their share to keep insects eaten. However — it makes vacuuming very precarious — for the spiders.

OCTOBER 4, Sunflower

Traveling along the highway in the fall of the year, I see the bright yellow flowers of the Jerusalem artichoke, or sunflower, rising like miniature suns above roadside thickets and fence rows; they seem to stand as signposts.

The Jerusalem artichoke, often called the wild sunflower, is not to be confused with the true artichoke, from which it differs greatly, although both have one feature in common: edibility. Long before the Europeans came to America, the Indians cultivated it for its edible tubers, which are fleshy and sweet and high in food content. It was doubtless this plant that Lewis and Clark describe in their journal entry of April 9, 1805, traveling in what is now North Dakota: "When we stopped for dinner the squaw [Sacajawea] went out, and after penetrating with a sharp stick the holes of the mice [probably prairie dogs or possibly gophers] near some driftwood, brought to us a quantity of wild artichokes, which the mice collect and hoard in large numbers. The root is white, of an ovate form, from one to three inches long, and generally of the size of a man's finger, and two, four and sometimes six roots are attached to a single stalk." It seems hardly necessary to add that the early colonists, learning of the sunflower's many uses, planted it extensively. They cooked and ate it like the potato, they used it in soups, and made it into pickles by half-boiling it, then slicing it and placing the slices in vinegar. And as it is an extremely persistent plant when once established, we may safely assume wherever we find it growing wild that the spot was once an aboriginal or colonial farm.

This sunflower is a stout, erect, rough-hairy plant, from four to twelve feet tall, and branching at the top, with ovate, pointed saw-toothed leaves, flower heads about three inches broad, and tubers that taste not unlike celery root or salsify. As early as 1617 it was introduced into Europe, and a few years later Parkinson tells us that the roots in London had become plentiful and cheap. The Italians also adopted the artichoke and cultivated it under the name of the girasole artichoke (sunflower artichoke), which eventually became corrupted into Jerusalem, the name by which we know it today.

There are some sixty species of sunflowers (genus *Helianthus*), most of which occur in North America. They are rather coarse, hardy, annual or perennial herbs, very diverse in size and character, with alternate leaves, though sometimes opposite above, that are usually coarsely toothed, and with flowers in terminal heads, the heads from three to twelve inches across, the florets composing the heads being of two kinds: yellow ray florets and yellow, brown, or purple disk florets.

The tall or giant sunflower is common in swamps and on the borders of wet meadows. Another fairly common species is the ten-petaled sun-

August 23 —

Why do I feel the need to await and record the wildflowers as they appear —
as if they won't? Haven't they done so always? Or am I just afraid that some of these lovely flowers won't return? That would be a sad loss indeed. I enjoy these wildflowers so. Like a roll call —
I check them in and note even the commonest sunflower and daisy.

flower, a showy species found on the borders of copses and in low damp woods, and another is the woodland sunflower that occurs in thickets and along woodland borders. The common or garden sunflower, a native of our prairies, is now to be seen most everywhere in meadows, waste places, fence rows, and along roadsides.

The seeds of the common sunflower have long been used as food by the American Indians. In their journal, dated July 17, 1805, when they were along the Missouri River in western Montana, Lewis and Clark wrote: ". . . along the bottoms, which have a covering of high grass, we observe the sunflower blooming in great abundance. The Indians of the Missouri, more especially those who do not cultivate maize, make great use of the seed of this plant for bread, or in thickening their soup." Strangely enough the seeds are more appreciated in some countries of Europe than in our own. The seed yields 20 percent oil which may be used for cooking, burning, or for soapmaking and an oil cake is excellent food for cattle. The nutritious seeds are eaten by many different species of gamebirds, songbirds, and rodents.

March 29 —
I've spent the winter feeding birds. Under the sunflower feeder, the fallen seeds have germinated and sprouted. The house finch and chickadees have provided for their new crop — will transplant these to the fence line. Must be 50 or 60 sprouts!

OCTOBER 18, Owl

I was returning home having been to the local village for a bit of shopping when I was suddenly startled by a loud noise in nearby trees. Turning quickly I saw the form of a little gray owl glide swiftly and silently on expanded wings, finally to alight on a branch where it turned and faced me and looked at me with a baleful eye.

The screech owl is a small bird scarcely measuring eight inches tall. Its broad head and eyes are set wide apart, its brown and gray colors are fairly well mixed. And with its long pointed white beard between the converging dark stripes and dappled breast, it always reminds me of some forest gnome.

The eastern screech owl, to give it its full name, is usually an inhabitant of some old neglected orchard. There it can find a hollow in the heart of some old tree to serve as a retreat during the sunlight hours, which it lines with straw, leaves, and feathers for a nest of from three to nine white eggs. Invariably the hollow selected is near a running brook, for the little owl delights in its daily bath. The screech owl is a useful bird feeding primarily on mice and insects and not on young birds as many believe.

The eastern screech owl—the only small eastern owl with ear tufts, and which, incidentally, occurs in two color phases, red-brown and gray—is a common bird flitting at dusk along the roads and unfrequented byways. I have often met it on its nightly excursions when a swish of wings gave notice of its approach.

Many years ago Pliny described the screech owl as execrable and accursed and pronounced the bird as a prognosticator of some fearful calamities. Somehow the bird has inherited the reputation of being associated with dire doings. And even today many people think that the owl is an ill-omened bird and quake whenever they hear its plaintive, long drawn-out wail. It is true the cry carries a note of sadness, but it is actually a love song unappreciated except by those for whose ears it is especially intended. Thoreau was so impressed by its mournfulness that he wrote in his journal: "I love to hear their wailing, their doleful responses, trilled along the woodside.... They give me a new sense of vastness and mystery of nature which is the common dwelling of us both."

Found a roosting gray screech owl in hole of dead stump almost eye level. It stretched up thin, made his eyes slits to hide yellow iris and further camouflage itself — resembling the gray dead tree it sat in. Fluffed out its gray feathers and then just stayed that way — perhaps totally convinced it was hidden from sight — even though it remained.

A slightly injured screech owl that spent some time with me, sleeping on a log on my mantle. It recovered and was released in my orchard. Owl was sketched — fed mice and allowed to sleep in the sun. It would snap its bill at me if I ventured close — puff out every feather, head down, bobbing and weaving — a force to be reckoned with —

appeared to enjoy bathing in low dish. When soaking wet resembles two large yellow eyes — a set of feet and not much in between.

Owl became more aggressive as health improved — a good sign.

OCTOBER 31, White-footed Mouse

To many folks the word *mouse* is synonymous with the little grayish-brown animal that sometimes invades our homes.

And because we dislike mice, we are inclined to view all mice as loathsome—wrongly, for the white-foot of our woodlands is far from repulsive. On the contrary, I have found it an appealing little animal.

Dressed in a spotless robe of grayish-fawn set off by the pure white of its underparts, and with a natural grace and agility of movement that are in keeping with a trim form and the keen expression in its large black eyes, this mouse is undoubtedly the most attractive and interesting of our native species.

I have found the white-foot to be of gentle disposition and one of the most unsuspicious of living creatures. All in all I doubt if anyone can find a more delightful little animal in the wild unless it is the saucy, impish chipmunk.

The white-foot closely resembles its relative, the deer mouse. Do not expect to see white-foots during the daytime, for they are essentially nocturnal in habit, although I have seen them occasionally on cloudy days. And we should not expect to find them in fields and meadow either. Their home is in the woods, though I have seen them frequent shrubby pastures if fringed by dense hedgerows, and a white-foot has been known to enter a village and even pay a visit to one's garden or backyard. Evergreens and hardwoods, thickets of blueberry bushes, and dense hedgerows are all to its liking, and hence it is sometimes known as the wood mouse.

Its nest may be in a half-rotted stump, among hollow roots, or in the cavity of a venerable beech. The white-foot may, particularly in the winter, appropriate the abandoned nest of some bird, which it might deftly cap over with leaves or thistledown, serving as a snug retreat in which to sleep away the day.

There are times when the white-foot mouse may not even wait for winter, but may take possession of a nest in summer, often not waiting for the rightful owners to leave. Instead it may drive them out by eating the eggs of young birds, for this mouse is omnivorous and will not pass up a meal of any kind if one is offered. Trick or treat!

Sitting in woods. Hidden from sight and very quiet. It's late in the day—almost toward evening and about to leave. Heard a small rustle—a tiny woodland imp—a white-footed mouse came out from under a leaf onto a branch. Glad I stayed.

Like to search for the shed antlers of deer before they disappear — chewed away by mice, squirrels, and other small animals for calcium and other minerals over the long winter.

NOVEMBER 7, Hop Hornbeam Tree

Its retiring disposition and preference for living a more or less solitary existence in cool fertile places, in the shade of oaks, maples, and other large trees, make the hop hornbeam an obscure tree, more than it should be. The hop hornbeam has an ancient lineage, and traces of its leaves and fruit are found in the Eocene and Miocene rocks of Europe; in Tertiary times, it ranged to Greenland. To find a hop-bearing tree in our forests is an unexpected experience, and yet the fruit of the hop hornbeam so closely resembles that of the hop vine that the tree has been named for the vine.

The hop hornbeam is a small tree, with leaves much like those of the birch and its spray resembling that of the beech. The bark, however, is rather characteristic, being grayish brown, thin, and scaling off into narrow strips whose surfaces are covered with squarish scales. The twigs, which remind us of fine wires, stand out at right angles from the stem; in midsummer they are a smooth, shiny, and light orange, and then become a dark brown after the first winter. Today I saw a hop hornbeam, and thought one might (correctly) suspect it to be a relative of the birches. Its leaves certainly give us that impression. In the winter the slender branches develop green catkins that cluster in threes on the end of the twigs, where they await the coming of spring in the manner of the birches. In spring the staminate swing out like those of the birch blossoms, but the pistillate are not much in evidence; if one looks closely the red, forked tongue extending out for the pollen may be seen at the ends of leafy shoots.

As autumn passes into winter, the leaves turn yellow and fall, but the hoplike clusters of little pale green sacs still hang on, though grudgingly giving up one small seed balloon after another to the persistent November wind. The seeds are too small to interest the human consumer, who would not deign to take the time and patience to extract them from their casings, but these seeds are the delight of the rabbit, deer, grouse, and grosbeak, the pheasant and the bobwhite.

Birch family (Hornbeams)

Differences between hornbeam and hop hornbeam. Both trees found in forest — where I see the wild turkeys.

← Winter catkins

↑ Fall seeds

↑ Hop Hornbeam — Rough bark — brownish-gray.

↑ Seeds

↑ American Hornbeam — Smooth bark — bluish gray.

NOVEMBER 11, Fox

I doubt very much if any animal has entered the pages of the world's literature as frequently and as extensively as the fox, or has occurred so often in the folklore of the countryside.

As a boy I learned Aesop's fable of the fox and the grapes, perhaps the best known of his fox fables. Doubtless many also recall Grimm's story of the fox and the wolf. Undoubtedly the best known of all literary accounts of the fox is the medieval beast-epic satirizing contemporary life and events found in French, Dutch, and German literature. The English version is *Reynard the Fox,* Caxton's translation from the Dutch of *Roman de Renart,* published in 1479.

To what extent the word *fox* has entered our language can be seen from a glance at the dictionary or the television set. Nor does the fox need to be described. We seldom see the fox in its natural habitat, normally rolling farm land interspersed with sparsely wooded areas, streams, and marshes, for the fox is essentially a nocturnal animal. But this does not mean it is not abroad during the daylight hours. I have seen the fox at times hunting mice in the fields and meadows. Its ability to elude the hunter with a gun is proverbial and yet not surprising in view of its qualities of shrewdness and cunning. That the fox has a highly developed intellect becomes clear by observing how quickly it learns from watching the ways of man. In spite of being constantly persecuted it not only has been able to survive but also increase in numbers. Few of our wild animals regard man with as little awe as the fox.

Of course one reason for its survival is its varied diet; the fox will eat almost anything, plant or animal, dead or alive. And when the snow cover is deep in the winter and its usual food is hard to find, the fox will take to eating the dried grass stems that tower above the snow.

Those of us who live in the country have often heard the thin, querulous barking of the fox on a still November night. Even stranger is the weird scream of the male fox, probably the most sinister, unearthly wild animal call that can be heard in North America.

May 8 — Found a red fox den near an old abandoned farm. Fox kits out of den playing — saw five kits through the woods about 80 yards ahead frolicking. Eased in closer — they were somewhat tolerant — no parent foxes seen — but know they're here. Den on a sunny knoll. Crawled closer — at first they scrambled back down burrow but one by one they came back out again. They pounce like cats. Play tug-of-war games and drag one another around. Occasionally fox kits would stop and stare at me — but then continue playing — learning for times ahead.

Gray fox out on the edge of a wooded opening. Pounced on something — probably a mouse or rabbit. I usually see more red fox than the tree-climbing grays. Quite a bit of red on the gray fox, but his tail ends in black (tip). Red's tail tip is white. Gray fox has a nice pepper gray coat on its back.

NOVEMBER 15, Salamander

In ancient times the salamander was a mythical lizardlike animal that people believed could live in fire and quench it by the chill of its body. Pliny refers to it in his *Natural History*, but it was Paracelsus, the famed alchemist, who named the imaginary animal. We have our own salamanders, but they cannot live in fire. Nor are they lizards, which becomes quite obvious when a lizard and a salamander are compared. A salamander has a soft, moist skin whereas the skin of a lizard is covered with scales.

North America has a number of species of salamanders, the most common perhaps being the spotted salamander. This is a rather handsome animal with yellow spots adorning the glistening upper blue-back surface and the lower half of the sides, the lower surface being a dusky slate flecked with white. The spots are not actually yellow but a dull greenish-yellow to a brilliant orange, and are not scattered but are arranged in two somewhat irregular rows, one on either side of the middorsal line of the head, trunk, and tail. There are usually six spots on the head, but this number may vary from four to nine; on the trunk there may be from thirteen to twenty; and on the tail from six to nineteen. There is no visible difference in the size or arrangement of the spots in the sexes, but during the breeding season, when the adults are in the ponds, the general color of the male seems to be somewhat more pronounced and the spots a little lighter.

An adult salamander measures about six inches in length, usually slightly more. It has a stout body, a broad, flat head, fairly large and strong legs without toes on the front and five on the hind feet, and a tail that is about half the salamander's length. Compare a male and female of the same length: The male is slightly slenderer than the female, and the head of the female is somewhat broader, more convex above, and widest at about the angle of the jaws. Also note that the distance between the front and hind feet in the female is about one-third of its total length, and in the male is about one-fourth. The tail of the male is usually longer and slenderer than that of the female.

During the fall the spotted salamander may sometimes be seen abroad during the day. I have seen one this month, and there are records of its having been seen crawling over the snow in winter. But such winter appearances—at least in the northern part of its range—are unusual; as the weather becomes colder the salamander seeks a winter refuge beneath a rotting log, under a stump, or in a hole in the upper layers of the woodland leaf cover, where it remains until the following spring.

April 4 —
Spotted salamander — beautiful little creature by the pond. It is their breeding season, and I know I'm lucky to see this little jewel of the underground

It reappears in March or April, according to locality. As soon as the weather permits, it sets out for the nearest pond or quiet inlet of a stream where it will breed. It travels only at night, only when the temperature is above the freezing point, and only when it is raining, if rain has fallen during the day—though it may be stimulated by a rapid runoff of snow following a decided rise in temperature.

How does the salamander locate water some distance from its winter quarters? It is really no mystery: The animal can locate water by showing a positive response to gravity (positive geotropism) and by being sensitive to a moisture gradient in the air, and thus move downhill and head for conditions of increasing moisture.

As a rule the male salamanders arrive at the breeding pond a day or two before the females. Some ponds may contain hundreds of salamanders, and when they engage in a sort of nuptial dance the scene becomes spectacular and worth observing. Lack of space precludes a description of this dance, but during it the males deposit their spermatophores on submerged leaves or branches. They are vase-shaped masses of clear jelly with a flattened flangelike base, capped with a white woolly substance. They look much like glass push-pins, are one-quarter to one-half of an inch in height, and contain hundreds of spermatozoa. After the spermatophores have been deposited, the females crawl over them and take them into their cloacal chambers, where the spermatozoa fertilize the eggs when they are laid.

The female salamander lays her eggs only at night in firm compact masses that are more or less globular in shape. They measure from one and a half to slightly over three inches in diameter and are attached to some submerged object. Each egg is enclosed in an envelope of jelly, and the entire cluster is covered with a thick layer of the same material. The eggs hatch in two or three weeks or longer, depending on the temperature of the water, into greenish-yellow or greenish-brown slender larvae that have noticeably flattened heads and are about half an inch long. At the time of hatching, the eyes, balancers (which are later dropped), and gills are well developed, but the front toes are represented merely by elongated buds that show no evidence of toes.

The larvae remain in the ponds until they are mature and ready to become adults. The transformation usually occurs in late summer or early fall, though the length of the larval period depends on a number of factors. The actual transformation takes place within a relatively short time, and once the young salamanders have reached land they remain there except for a brief return to the water for breeding.

April 30 —
Seeing many red efts in the woods. It rained all weekend, and the little salamanders are everywhere — underfoot. I'm nervous about walking and stepping on them.

One scene I'm seeing over and over is an eft on a bed of moss at the base of a tree or on a log. I keep picking them up to look closer — can't help myself.

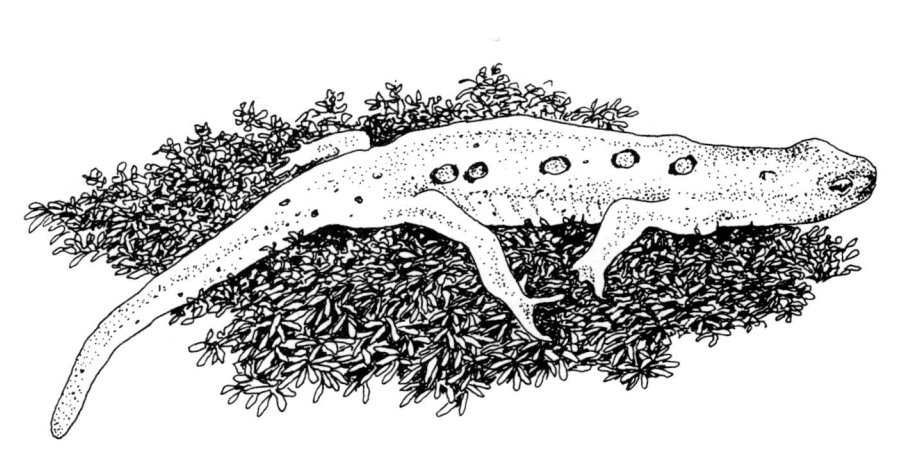

NOVEMBER 19, Acorn

As a boy of about nine, I remember collecting acorns during the fall of the year. I would pick them off the ground and fill my pockets with them—to no purpose that I can remember, except to fulfill a boy's penchant for collecting.

At that time the role of acorns in the scheme of nature didn't mean much to me. I knew little about them, except that they were nuts and that squirrels buried them to recover and eat when winter came and food became scarce. It was not until years later that I learned through botanical studies that acorns are not the common things they seem to be. They are the characteristic fruit of the oak family, of course, and not found in any other family of plants. But more than that, they have an individuality of their own. Acorns are variable in size, shape, and in other characteristics that hold true for the species, so that any acorn may serve to identify a species of oak tree. Who doesn't know the acorns of the red oak or the mossy oak?

An acorn is a nut. A nut, botanically speaking, is a hard one-seeded fruit, and an acorn is usually seated in a woody cup of indurated bracts, the cup itself also being variable in the different species. Acorns take one or two years to mature and this has led to the oaks being divided into two groups: those that ripen acorns the first year, and those that ripen them the second year. The annual-fruited oaks have leaves with rounded lobes and sinuses and generally also have pale bark, hence they are known as the white oak group. The biennial-fruited oaks have dark-colored bark and their leaves have lobes that end in angles tipped with bristly points; these oaks are known as the black oak group. Any acorn found on the twigs of an oak during the winter or spring must obviously belong to the black oak group. Because these nuts are not mature it would be difficult to identify this oak group from the nuts alone; one must rely on the cup, whose characteristics are fully developed.

I have never been able to understand why we haven't made more use of acorns as food. People in Asia eat them; so did the early colonists in America; and, of course, the Indians gathered them in large quantities for winter use. The Indians ground the nuts into a sort of flour out of which they baked bread. They also roasted the acorns, ground them, and eventually prepared the product as a beverage. In 1620 the Pilgrims found baskets of roasted acorns that the Indians had hidden in the ground. In his *Travels* William Bartram wrote that the acorn of the live oak is "small, but sweet and agreeable to the taste when roasted. . . . the Indians obtain from it a swet oil, which they use in the cooking of hominy, rice, etc; and they also roast it in hot embers, eating it as we do chestnuts." The Indians also used the acorns of the live oak to thicken their "venison-soop." "They likewise draw an Oil, very pleasant and wholesome, little inferior to that of almonds." So wrote Mark Catesby more than two hundred years ago.

The acorns that the New England Indians roasted were doubtless those of the white oak; they are sweet-flavored and found acceptance by the Pilgrims, who not only ate them but found that the acorn had other good qualities: "By boyling it long, it giveth an oil which they keep to supple their joynts." They skimmed the oil from the water before they ate the nuts remaining in the pot.

Acorns have been an article of human consumption since time immemorial. The tribes of the Near East as long ago as 20,000 B.C. ate them.

Both wild and domestic animals feed extensively on acorns. For centuries pigs and hogs have been fed on acorns; indeed the domestication of the pig was not brought about until humans began to realize that they had to invest some of their own food in the rearing of the pig. One of these items was the acorn. This was about 7000 B.C.

Despite what is to us a bitter taste, bears seem inordinately fond of the acorns of the bear or scrub oak and become quite fat on them. Squirrels and other rodents store acorns for winter use, though few are perhaps aware that a California woodpecker also indulges in the practice. Acorns are an important source for wildlife because they are nutritious and also because they usually constitute an abundant available staple. In years when acorns are scarce, as sometimes happens, many species of wildlife may be hard-pressed for sustenance.

Birds too—the jays and woodpeckers, as well as quail and ducks—include acorns in their diet. Ducks feed principally on the comparatively small acorns of the water oak and willow oak which grow near ponds and streams. Wild turkeys also eat acorns, swallowing them whole regardless of size.

Bears and squirrels, the raccoon, peccary, and deer, all appear to have a taste for acorns—especially those of the white oak group, which seem to be preferred over those of the black oak group by wildlife in general, as they were by the early settlers and the Indians.

And after all that November feasting, there still remain enough acorns to begin a new generation of oak trees the following spring.

October 13 — Went for a walk in a nearby hemlock and oak woodlot. Lots of limestone here — some high formations. Largest wild ginger I've seen — many acorns — and chipmunks. Herds of chipmunks scampering everywhere — two almost ran into me. They squalk, scramble, and chatter at one another while they stuff their cheeks with acorns. I can imagine the contest for acorns in each chipmunk burrow. The fury to collect. Partridgeberry — pipsissewa and hundreds of hemlock seedlings here.

October 14 — The woods are nice — the smell of October. Good acorn mast — dropping like rain. Leaves falling like the song. Sun dancing everywhere — birds moving — a whole set changing like the theater. Wild turkeys coming they have incredible hearing and eye sight — I can't move or make a sound. There are several birds scratching up this feast of acorns on an oak knoll through the woods. Turkeys are noisy — some of the toms occasionally gobble as though it's spring. Others are bickering, establishing order.

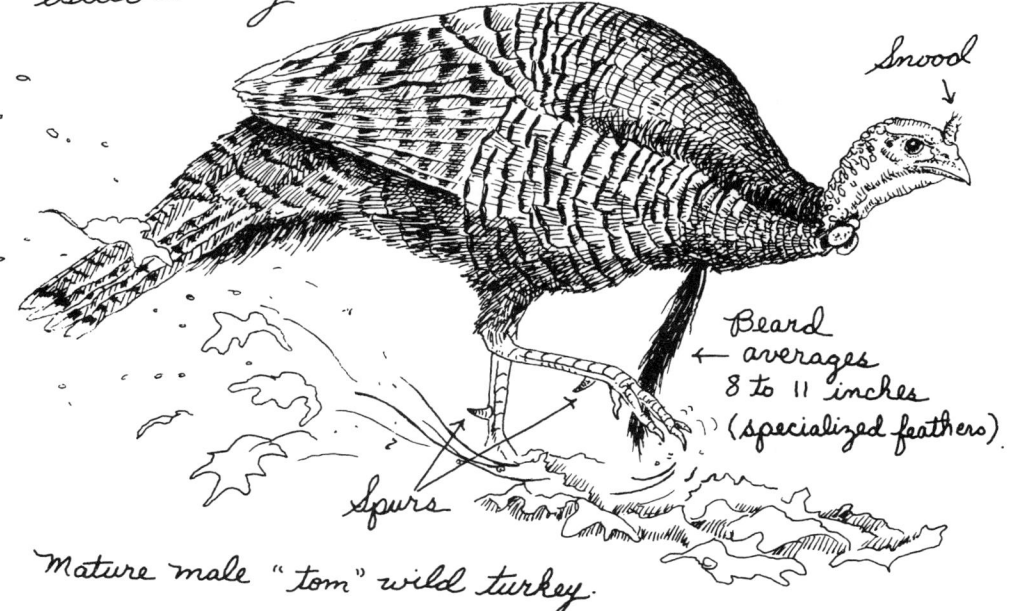

Snood

Beard averages 8 to 11 inches (specialized feathers).

Spurs

Mature male "tom" wild turkey.

NOVEMBER 25, Moth

Moths are normally night-flying insects of summer; and one would hardly expect to see them in the fall of the year. But go into the woods in November or December and you may be startled to see moths flying about among the leafless trees during the daytime, appearing like so many tiny ghosts. The American entomologist Harris, writing as long ago as 1862, commented on this winter appearance of moths: "In mild and open winters I have seen them in every month from October to March. . . . They begin to make their appearance after the first hard frosts in the autumn, usually towards the end of October, and they continue to come forth, in greater or smaller numbers, according to the mildness or severity of the weather after the frosts have begun."

These moths are brownish-gray with a wing expanse of an inch or more, the forewings rather glossy with purple reflections and crossed by two jagged whitish bands that are, however, sometimes so faint that they

November 13 — In the woods.

Male fall cankerworm — female does not fly — wingless.

Female crawling on trunk of tree where she will lay her eggs.

can hardly be seen. The hindwings are grayish-brown, each with a faint black dot.

The flying moths are the males of the fall cankerworm, and when we see them they are in search of the females. Both males and females have recently emerged from their cocoons in the ground, but the females (which are much the same color as the males) are wingless and hence cannot fly; they must wait patiently for the males to find them on the trees, up which they have climbed and where they will lay their eggs after mating.

As a rule, the females lay their eggs shortly after the nuptial event has taken place, though sometimes they wait until spring. They place several hundred eggs side by side in several rows in a compact mass on the smaller twigs and branches of almost any deciduous tree, the eggs being securely fastened with a strong gluey secretion and covered with gray hairs that they rub from their bodies. To the naked eye the eggs look like tiny gray flower pots, but through a hand lens they appear cut off at the top, with a central puncture and a brown circle near the border of the disk. They are decidedly worth looking for on a November afternoon.

June 6 —

Gypsy moths (caterpillars) are becoming more apparent — can hear their "rain" of droppings all around me in the woods. Male moth flies. During bad infestation years see more cuckoos. These birds seem to readily eat the hairy caterpillars.

Caterpillar

Male — brown

Female — white larger than male — usually lays eggs on tree trunks near ground.

DECEMBER 1, Trout

Spring and summer have always been the traditional seasons for fishermen. It is then that along the banks of fast-moving streams, beside still ponds, from boats and bridges, you can see people dangling lines from outstretched poles or casting hopefully for some unseen prey beneath the waters. But very few of these hopeful anglers think of the full seasons of the fish life cycle. To them often fish are spring and summer creatures with no past and no future. And yet winter is for many local fish species perhaps the most critical season in their life cycle.

A good example of this is the life of the popular sport fish, the brook trout. When the lower temperatures of autumn signal the approach of winter and the water of streams and lakes begins to cool, brook trout begin to migrate toward their spawning grounds. Trout that have spent the summer in streams journey up-current, and those that have lived in lakes enter inflowing streams. At this time of the year the two sexes differ remarkably in appearance. The sides of the male are a flaming red, the lower jaw becomes hooked upward, the teeth grow larger, and the body becomes more flattened. The female remains relatively unchanged except that her body increases somewhat in size as her eggs develop.

Following a period of courtship, mating occurs and the eggs, which may not hatch for three months or more depending on the temperature of the water, are deposited in the nest or redd, a shallow basin excavated in the bottom of the stream by the female.

The brook trout is not the only freshwater fish that breeds in the winter. The whitefish may breed as early as November, though its eggs may not hatch until the following spring. In the first few weeks of December, the lake herring move into shallows in great numbers and leave their eggs on the bottom; when the spring sun has warmed the water sufficiently, they will hatch. And as soon as the ice clears, the familiar yellow perch may move into their spawning grounds in the shallows along pond and lake shores. Although these freshwater fish are not in the true sense winter breeders, their breeding periods nevertheless do extend over a considerable part of the winter season. This is to their advantage, as the young fry are thus able to get a good start in early spring before competition for survival becomes too keen.

In general freshwater fish are not as lively in winter as in the warmer months, although the species vary considerably in the extent of their activity. It is questionable if any of them hibernate in the true sense of the word, and yet there are some whose activity is greatly reduced. The rock bass, the small-mouthed bass, the large-mouthed bass, and the bullheads

December 4 — It's been a mild winter up to now — not much snow and not too cold.

My brook is running good, and I see a brook trout.

Not only is it a colorful fish — it's one of the best tasting.

rest quietly on the bottom of the lakes and streams or hide among the leaves or rocks, eating very little. The common carp is believed to eat little or nothing at all and may burrow in the mud—although carp can be caught in seines lowered through holes in the ice, which would seem to indicate that some of them, at least, remain active.

Some fish, such as the yellow perch, pickerel, pike, sunfish, and suckers, move about freely beneath the ice, feed more or less regularly, and may be caught with a line suspended through an opening in the ice. The brook trout also remain more or less active throughout the winter, though in the coldest weather they remain in the still pools and backwaters or beneath the banks. That brook trout is lurking in my favorite brook on December 1 as well as April 1.

Common sense tells us that the food supply of our native freshwater fish is not quite as plentiful in winter as in summer, and yet there appears to be enough to sustain these species. The pickerel feeds chiefly on small fish and insects; the yellow perch on crustaceans, insects, and small fish; the black-nosed dace on insects, small crustaceans, algae, and herb plant material; and the brook trout on insects, crayfish, snails, clams, and occasionally salamanders. As a rule plants and animals grow more slowly at low temperatures than at high temperatures, and this is also true of fish. One can observe this periodic check on growth by examining the scales of fish; the ridges are more crowded together and incomplete when growth is retarded. Such a region of crowded ridges, known as a year mark, is formed in winter.

January 23 —
The whole county is frozen. The lake ice is safe, and ice fishing is in full progress.
Yellow perch taking bait. Wind is blowing — my feet are cold. A family outing on the lake to ice fish.

Yellow perch

DECEMBER 6, Skunk

Slowly following a winding path through the woods today, I made a turn and was suddenly brought up short—for there in front of me sat a skunk. One more step and I would either have stepped on or walked into it, and I would have been *persona non grata* in my own household. But as it turned out the skunk apparently had not seen me, for a moment or two later it moved on. I waited while the skunk got far enough ahead of me before I resumed my own walk.

Many of our native animals have an undeserved bad reputation because of an ancient superstition or a misconception of some trait or form of behavior. And the skunk is a case in point. For the skunk is probably the most misunderstood of all our native wild animals. Instinctively we shy away as if it were some loathsome thing, and yet there is probably no animal more harmless or inoffensive.

It is true that at times the skunk may offend our sensibilities, but he does not do so intentionally. I would not be surprised if the skunk itself dislikes the odor of the powerful effluvium that it ejects in time of stress. Is the skunk careful not to get any of it on itself? Most likely. For the skunk is actually neat and meticulous in personal habits and, moreover, always minds its own business.

With its handsome coat of glistening black, set off with two broad white stripes, and its large and bushy tail, carried like a flag, the skunk makes a striking appearance. It might even be called handsome. The skunk's front legs, however, are very much shorter than the hind ones, giving it a very peculiar gait, but these features doubtless serve it in some way.

The skunk is mainly nocturnal in habits, and during the night often visits my gardens and back yard for something to eat. Its movements are quite deliberate and without haste, for the skunk is perfectly fearless of other animals, including humans (including me).

If encountered and left alone, it will continue on its way with a genteel and dignified indifference. But the skunk's relative immunity from attack by other animals has made it careless and more than once has proved its undoing, since it has never learned to avoid a trap or the dangers of the highway.

As it ambles along, the skunk carries its tail at a slight elevation. The moment danger threatens the tail is raised still higher, so that the long hairs hang drooping like a long plume. Here is a conspicuous and unmistakable hint that the skunk will tolerate no interference. Should an animal fail to take the hint, the back is arched and the feet stamped as a

One mustn't drop a bag of trash on the head of a resident trash can skunk — in the dark. The skunk reacted without a moment's notice. It was, after all, scared out of its wits. His spray of defense took my breath away while he made a hasty retreat. The odor took my family's breath away too when I tried to go back inside — much loud and leg-slapping laughter was coming from the house as I left my belongings in the barn — forever!

final warning. The skunk then discharges the powerful fluid, for which it is so well known, being careful to lift its tail high above its back so that he himself will not be defiled.

The odorous fluid is stored in two glands located just under the tail, and may be ejected a distance of ten feet. It is yellow in color, somewhat phosphorescent, and resembles musk in its extraordinary volatility. Intensely acid, it produces a burning sensation. The discharge at any time is scarcely three drops, yet this small quantity will scent the air for half a mile or more in any direction.

Helping to assist an injured great horned owl. This owl reeks of skunk smell — no doubt a recent meal. Great horned owl has a varied diet and has been known to dine on skunk — or anything else it chooses.

DECEMBER 10, Bayberry

"It yields a pleasant fragrance to all," wrote Robert Beverly in his *History of Virginia* as he described bayberry candles, manufactured by the American colonists from a stiff, crooked shrub, found growing along the coastal plain from Nova Scotia to Florida and Alabama.

The bayberry is a shrub three to eight feet high, with a brownish-gray bark and elliptical, leathery leaves that are broadest at the tip. The leaves are pale green tinged with red that darkens to a bronze-purple in autumn, and the flowers occur in catkins. The fruit is a dry, waxy, gray-white drupelike nut and is used in the making of bayberry candles. The fruit has a balsamic odor. The odor comes also from new shoots and the undersurface of leaves. It originates from minute, transparent dots that occur on shoots and leaves.

The wax used in making candles is obtained by boiling the "berries" in water. The wax rises to the surface and hardens on cooling. It is said that about one-third of the weight of the "berries" consists of wax.

Our native shrubs, whose colorful fruits attract our eye and whose various uses our forefathers devised, seem particularly prominent to me during the holiday season. A number of these shrubs had important uses for the early Americans. One was the bayberry whose wax had a commercial value. Another was the New Jersey tea, whose leaves were used as a tea substitute. The New Jersey tea is a shrubby plant, common in open woods and thickets, with coarse, woody, brown-green or bronzy upright stems, one to three feet high, and alternate ovate three-ribbed leaves, pointed at the apex and often heart-shaped at the base. The flowers appear in May or early June, and are small, white, and lightly odorous. They are arranged in cone-shaped plumy clusters on long stems from the leaf angles. The shrub is quite conspicuous when in bloom and is most attractive and decorative. The fruits are small three-lobed capsules containing three pale brown seeds.

It is said that when the oriental tea brought to the American colonies in English vessels became unpopular, its use considered unpatriotic, colonial housewives began collecting the leaves of the New Jersey tea, dried them, and then brewed a tea. Doubtless many a tired American soldier found it refreshing when camping at Valley Forge. The plant has also been found useful in furnishing a red dye obtained from the roots; hence the New Jersey tea also has been known as the redroot.

Another shrub, whose leaves have been used in making a tea is the spicebush that gilds the swampy March or April woods with knots of golden-yellow flowers. Spicy, aromatic in bark, leaves, and fruit, the spicebush is a shrub seven to fifteen feet high, with smooth dark-brown bark, slender brittle twigs, oval or oblong dark-green leaves, and bright-scarlet, oval drupes that are relished by thrushes. In earlier days the shrub was used in preparing various medicines, but whether it had any medicinal virtue appears doubtful. But there has never been any doubt as to its value as a tea; not only the leaves but also the twigs and bark have been used in making the beverage. Michaux, the French botanist, while traveling in the American wilderness wrote in his journal (February 1796) of stopping at a settler's cabin. "I had supped the previous evening on tea made from the shrub called Spicewood. A handful of young twigs or branches is set to boil and after it has boiled at least a quarter of an hour, sugar is added and it is drunk like tea. I was told that milk makes it much more agreeable to the taste. This beverage restores strength, and it has that effect, for I was very tired when I arrived."

Other native shrubs whose dried leaves have been used in preparing tea are Labrador tea, Appalachian tea, and sweet fern. Labrador tea is a beautiful evergreen shrub, from one to three feet high, found in swamps, bogs, and damp woods. It has slender, light-brown ascending stems, extremely velvety-haired twigs, small, leathery oblong, entire leaves that when crushed give off a pleasant tealike fragrance. The flowers are small, white in terminal clusters, each with a five-toothed calyx, a corolla of five spreading petals, and five stamens. The flower develops into five-celled capsules. Despite the fact that the leaves are resinous, astringent, and bitter, it is said that they too were used as a tea substitute during the Revolutionary War.

A plant that looks like a fern, grows like a bush, and is familiar to all who know the outdoors, the sweet fern is a fragrant, round-headed shrub about two feet high. It grows on hillsides, stony uplands, and dry pastures. It has a dull-red or dark-brown woody stem. The leaves are very narrow, almost linear, the margins cut into many rounded lobes, dark green, stalked, and very fragrant when crushed. The flowers are small, inconspicuous and green, the fruit burlike, pale or rusty green, and also very aromatic when crushed.

A relative of the sweet fern, the sweet gale, has spicy leaves that have been used to give a pleasant flavor to roasts. Occurring in swamps and pond margins, it has dark brown, ascending stems, wedge-shaped leaves, and flowers in catkins. The fruit is resinously waxy, berrylike, and crowded in a cluster of two to six nutlets. The leaves of the sweet bay, a shrub of wet and swampy places, also have been used to flavor roasts and gravies, and from the creamy white flowers a perfume has been made.

Occurring on the sea beaches and sand dunes, the beach plum is a low shrub with a straggling habit, with crooked brown stems, olive-green leaves, and white flowers in profuse clusters that are followed by equally

April 24 —
Spicebush flowers out next to my brook. Appear very yellow in contrast to other shrubs just opening with small leaves.

Under the spicebush are trout lilies, dandelions, and two shades of violets — all in bloom. Spicebush as usual is fragrant and pleasant smelling — reminds me of citrus.

profuse clusters of handsome, globular, purple or scarlet fruits. They are collected and sold in local markets as they are excellent for preserving and for making jelly.

The cranberry is common in stores, but few have seen it in its native home in the bogs and marshes of northeastern United States. There are essentially two species of wild cranberries, the large and the small. The American or large cranberry is the commercial cranberry. It is a slender, straggling shrub growing from six inches to two feet long with ascending branches, entire evergreen leaves, pale rose-colored flowers, and oblong or nearly round berries, at first green but later red. The small cranberry is a smaller species with slender, erect stems, olive-green leaves, and with similar, though smaller, flowers and berries.

The name cranberry is said originally to have been *craneberry* because the curve of the branches appeared like the neck of the crane. The Indians, it is believed, showed the Pilgrims how to prepare the berries for the table. Because the berries kept so well, ten barrels of them were sent to King Charles II as a gift, but whether in an eating condition after the slow voyage by sailing vessel is not known.

When I walk along almost any roadside in midsummer I will find another shrub called the elder, "foamed over with blossoms white as spray." Later the elder will stand bowed under its burden of purple berries. The round and juicy berries are not quite to our taste when eaten raw, but are excellent in pies and puddings. Elderberry wine is said to have medicinal properties. The elder is an attractive shrub that in blossom equals in beauty the finest garden ornamentals.

Probably few native shrubs are as useful as the blueberries. There are a number of species, the two most important being the dwarf blueberry or low sweet blueberry of sandy or rocky soil and the high-bush blueberry, probably the finest of them all. The dwarf blueberry can be distinguished from other blueberries by its close bunches of light-blue, very sweet berries that grow near the ends of the branches attended by many leaves. The dwarf berries are among the finest of wild fruits, sweet and juicy, and excellent for pies, puddings, and desserts in general. Much relished by the Indians, because of their abundance they were an important item in their diet. They are the early-market blueberry.

The high-bush blueberry is the late-market blueberry. It is a tall species, three to thirteen feet high, of swamps, wet meadows, and thickets, with spreading greenish-brown branches, white flowers suffused with pink, and bluish-black berries. In autumn the shrub becomes a most brilliant scarlet, a veritable burning bush of swamps and meadows.

July 22 —
Turkey scratchings here —
wild turkey droppings are
"blueberry blue" — the turkeys are
eating ripened blueberries heavily all
through this area.
It's a first
come/first served
law of nature when
the berries are
ready!

DECEMBER 15, Pine

To many people every evergreen tree (or perhaps more specifically any conifer) is without distinction a pine, whether such a tree is a pine, spruce, balsam, fir, or some other relative. The pines and their relatives are a familiar feature of the landscape, but at no season are they as beautiful as when laden with snow, or my favorite Christmas ornaments. And as the snow deepens and food becomes increasingly scarce, the food the evergreens provide in the form of bark, leaves, and seeds is above even the deepest blanket of snow and thus available to a variety of birds and mammals.

The pines have an ancient lineage, being survivors from a prehistoric age when their contemporaries were the lycopods, the sigillarids, and the cycads whose remains formed the coal deposits. The visible signs that serve to distinguish the pines and their relatives from other trees hint little of the structural differences that separate them from their companions of the present-day forest. The architecture of a pine flower is simplicity itself and typical of the plants that formed the vegetation of the earth in the distant past. Look at a pine flower today; you are looking back in time some millions of years.

The fruit of the pine is a cone, and hence the tree is called a conifer or cone-bearer. So, too, is the fruit of the spruce, fir, and hemlock, and hence these trees are also known as conifers, as are the red cedar, yew, and juniper though their fruit is berry. All the conifers are commonly known as evergreens because their leaves remain on the branches throughout the winter (with two exceptions, however, the larch and the bald cypress).

The conifers, a hardy group, are at their best on mountain slopes and highlands, where other trees are unable to survive the rigors of winter. They are also able to grow on sandy, rocky, or otherwise poor soil not suitable for other tree growth. There are some five hundred million acres of forest in the United States today and, of the trees that constitute this vast area of plant life, the conifers are by far the most abundant. No one can deny that they are one of our major natural resources or dispute their value in furnishing building materials, pulp wood, and a number of other products. And Christmas trees.

Put a white-tailed deer out of his day bed in an old hemlock grove. Snow hardly melted in bed, so well is the insulating quality of the hollow hairs of his winter coat keeping him warm. Coat also changes from reddish brown to drab gray, matching the color of the winter woods.

White pine has 5 needles.

pine needles →

cone ↓

In the fall, the tree sheds ochre-colored needles that lie beneath in "a bed of needles."

December 24 —
White pine tree in the field bent and burdened with last night's heavy snow — beautiful. Last spring we planted this field with seedling Christmas trees.

DECEMBER 27, Goldfinch

One of the interesting facets of the nature scene during the winter is seeing a flock of goldfinches suddenly appear from nowhere and descend on a wind-swept field. As they meticulously search for seeds on the dried and withered stalks, which in the bright sunshine trace delicate and intricate shadows on the snow, their notes fall on the frosty air like the tinkle of a thousand bells, wishing me a happy New Year.

Sometimes they exhibit a habit common to birds that gather together. The entire flock progresses in one direction across the field, the birds in the rear successively flying to the front, over the heads of the others, apparently seeking an advantage over them. But this aggressive rivalry, if such it can be called, does not appear to be resented; the flock always seems to associate with one another in a spirit of harmony and friendliness. There is an undefinable charm to these gatherings, perhaps enhanced by the fact that at any moment the entire flock may suddenly whirl up and fly away, quickly to be lost in the distance, out of sight and hearing.

The American goldfinch is one of the most distinctive birds of the countryside. Seen throughout the year, it is always cheerful, rarely giving voice to harsh sound, and travels in company with others of its kind, in flocks of varying size. As I observe them flying restlessly from one place to another, constantly giving voice to their characteristic notes, I get the impression that they are high-spirited, fun-loving birds. Bradford Torrey has given us this picture of the goldfinch: "Our American Goldfinch is one of the loveliest of birds. With his elegant plumage, his rhythmical, undulatory flight, his beautiful song, and his more beautiful soul, he ought be one of the best beloved, if not one of the most famous; but he has never yet had half his deserts." We have never taken the goldfinch into our hearts as we have the chickadee, the robin, and the bluebird, and I half suspect it is because this bird so much prefers the company of its own kind.

When we come upon a lone goldfinch, it seems lost and out of its element. At such a time, it gives out its long sweet call as if to attract the attention of companions, all the while looking about and listening for them. When it sees them or hears their voices, it goes bounding away with joy to join them.

In winter the male goldfinch is drab in color, but when the green of spring begins to tint the fields and woods it becomes panoplied in jet and gold. Throughout the succeeding weeks, flocks of varying size may be observed flying from place to place, from field to wooded tract, wandering happily about, feasting on various seeds, insects, the buds of apple trees, and other dainties, and singing blithely in trees and on telephone wires.

Winter goldfinches — joyous flight!

Then as the summer advances and thistledown, with which the goldfinch characteristically lines its nest, becomes available, their thoughts turn to more serious matters: to courtship, nest building, and the rearing of their young. But that is months from now; for the present, on the edge of a new year, heading eventually, inexorably toward a new spring, I am content just to see them and to hear their calls. A thousand bells.

December 29 — A cloudy afternoon — a small group of goldfinch are feeding on evening primrose by the edge of a dirt road. All the milkweed pods are silvery gray now, and most have spread their seeds on the wind — a new generation of milkweed. Everything has a winter brown-and-gray look, the brilliant autumn colors having been frosted away on the cold nights. Even the goldfinch are wearing dull winter clothes — not the bright yellow and black of the male in spring. Winter is beginning — bringing this year to a close — but nature is always renewing, and I look forward to another spring....

INDEX

acorns, 214–17
   as food, 214–15
aggregate fruits, 134
alder tree, 56
American copper butterfly, 120
American dagger caterpillar, 167
American elm tree, 8, 55
   flowering of, 74
American robin, 187
American toad, 151
American wild mint, 83
anglewing butterfly, 119
animals
   and acorns, 215–17
   one-celled, 8
   and shadblow berries, 72
   and sumac seed heads, 181, 183
   in winter, 8
   See also specific animals
ants, and spring azure butterfly caterpillar, 43
aphids, ladybugs and, 49
Appalachian tea, 229
apple blossoms, 53
apple tree, 8, 55
Arethusa (orchid), 96
aspen tree, 55, 56
asters, 116, 165–66, 178
autumn foliage, 80, 180

bagworm, 23
bald cypress tree, 233
Baltimore butterfly, caterpillars of, 170
banded purple butterfly, 119
bark, as food for animals, 5
barred owl, 31
bayberry, 228
beach grass seeds, 5
beach plum, 229, 231
bear swamp, 28, 31
beaver lodge, 14
beaver ponds, 14, 60, 62, 188
beebread, 46, 48
beech tree, 180
   flowering of, 59
bees, 85
beetles, 5
   Donacia, 147
berries, botanical definition of, 134
Beverly, Robert, 228
birch tree, 55, 56, 59, 130–32
   fungus, 131
birds
   backyard, 187–92
   bobcats and, 12
   goldfinches, 236–39
   loons, 153–55
   and shadblow berries, 72
   and sumacs, 181
   and sunflower seeds, 198
   whippoorwill, 156–57
   in winter, 1–2, 3–5, 6, 7, 8, 15–22, 40–41
   woodpecker, 103–4
   See also specific birds
black bear den, 58
black birch tree, 10, 59, 132
black raspberry, 137
black swallowtail butterfly, 122
black willow tree, 56
black-capped chickadee, 187
black-nosed dace, 222
blackberry, 134, 135, 136, 137, 138

INDEX

blazing star, 178
blister beetle, 163
blue beech tree. *See* hornbeam
blue butterfly, 120
    caterpillars of, 169
blue cedar tree berries, 34
blue flag iris, 81
blue jay, 1, 5, 15–18, 189
blue-stemmed goldenrod, 161
blueberries, 231, 232
bluebirds, 42, 44, 187
bluebottle flies, 23
bobcats, 12, 13
    tracks of, 12, 14
bog goldenrod, 161
bog turtle, 111
brambles, 134–38
British soldier lichens, 60
broad-lipped twayblade, 96
broadwing hawks, 185
brook trout, 220–23
brown creeper, 100
brown snake, 98, 99, 102
brown-tail moth caterpillar, 168
brown thrasher, 190
brownie cap mushroom, 144
Bryant, William Cullen, 178
Bryozoans, and waterlilies, 147
buckeye butterfly, 120
bufflehead, 8
bulbous buttercup, 87
bullhead, 220, 222
bumblebee, 46–48, 163
    and jewelweed, 112–13
bur marigold, 178
Burroughs, John, 32
buttercups, 87–89
butterflies, 118–24
    distinctive habits and behavior patterns, 120–21
    habitats of, 119
    See also specific butterflies

cabbage butterfly, 122, 124
    chrysalides of, 23
caddis fly, larvae of, 23
Calopogon (orchid), 96
camouflage
    and blue jay, 15
    and junco, 21
Canada goose, 81
candles, bayberry, 228
cardinals (bird), 1, 189, 190
cardinals (flower), 112
Carolina wren, 131
carp, 222
carpenter bee, 163
catbirds, 189
cats, compared with bobcats, 12

caterpillars, 15, 167–71
    food plants of, 170–71
    hairs of, 167–68
    protective systems of, 168–69
    of spring azure butterfly, 43
Catesby, Mark, 215
catkins, 56, 59, 130, 132
cattail moths, larvae of, 23
cattails, 158–60
Cecropia moth
    caterpillar of, 171
    pupae of, 23
cedar waxwing, 188–89
Chalcid fly, 163
chanterelle mushroom, 144
chickadees, 3, 4, 5, 181, 198
chickweed, 178
chipmunks, 82, 216
chokecherries, 161
Christmas fern, 8
Christmas tree, 233
Cleistogamous flowers, 113
cloudberries, 134
cloudless sulphur butterfly, 124
club mosses, 8
cockspur, 80
coleus, 85, 86
colorational antigeny, 124
columbine, 34
common naucoria mushroom, 144
common tree frog, 68
conifers, 233–35
Coprinus mushroom, 144
coral honeysuckle, 112
coral mushroom, 145
cottontail rabbit, 135
cottony-cushion scale, 49–50
countershading, 21
cowbird, 188
cowper, 176
crabgrasses, 80
cradle-cocoon, 23
cranberry, 231
crayfish, 172–75
    as aquarium pet, 175
creeping buttercup, 87–88
cricket, 5, 176–77
    chirping by, 176–77
    as pet, 177
crow, 2
cuckoo, and gypsy moth caterpillar, 219
cutworm, as food for toad, 152

daisy fleabane, 178
dandelions, 77–79, 230
dark-eyed junco, 19
day lilies, 84
decapods, 172
deer antlers, 204

deer mice, 5, 202
DeKay, James Edward, 98
destroying angel mushroom, 144
dewberry, 134, 137
dioecious tree, 55
diving beetle, 23
dog, bobcat and, 12
dogwood tree, 55
downy rattlesnake plantain, 96
downy woodpecker, 101
dragonfly, 125–29
drupelets, 134
dusky meadow brown butterfly, 119
Dutch elm disease, 75
dwarf blueberry, 231

early blooming columbine, 112
early goldenrod, 161
eastern cottonwood tree, 56
eastern screech owl, 199–201
eggs
    of brook trout, 220
    of cabbage butterfly, 122, 124
    of crayfish, 173, 175
    of cricket, 176
    of dragonflies, 125
    of fall cankerworm, 219
    of gypsy moth, 219
    of painted terrapin, 110
    of salamander, 212
    of spring peeper, 61–62
    of sunfish, 90, 92
    of swallowtails, 122
    of woodpeckers, 103
    See also insects, eggs of; larvae
elder tree, 231
elderberry wine, 231
elm tree, 56, 74–76
    insect eggs on, 23
epistylis, 8
evening primrose, 239

fairy-ring mushroom, 144
fall cankerworm, 218–19
fall webworm, 169, 170
field cricket. See cricket
fir tree, 233
fish, breeding in winter, 220
    See also specific fish
flood control, and cattails, 158
flowers
    of black raspberry, 137
    butterflies and, 119
    of cattail, 158
    of raspberries, 136
fly amanita mushroom, 144
flying squirrel, 141–43

food
    acorns as, 214–15
    of blue jays, 15
    of bobcats, 12
    of caterpillars, 170–71
    of cattail, 158
    cattail root as, 158
    of crayfish, 172–73
    of crickets, 177
    of fox, 207
    of freshwater fish in winter, 222
    of painted terrapin, 108
    of red squirrel, 105, 107
    of shrew, 28
    sunflower as, 196
    sunflower seeds as, 198
    of toads, 152
    of winter birds, 3, 5
fossils, of prehistoric dragonfly, 126–27
fox, 8, 207–9
foxtail, 80
fringed polygala, 65
fritillary butterfly, 119, 120
frog, 61–68
    See also gray tree frog; green frog;
        leopard frog; pickerel frog; spring
        peeper; wood frog
fruit orchards, grackles and, 40

garden sunflower, 198
garter snake, 102
gaywing. See fringed polygala
Gerardia, 178
giant sunflower, 196
giant white puffball mushroom, 146
gill-over-the-ground, 83
gnat, 23
golden garden spider, 195
golden-crowned kinglet, 32, 33
goldenrods, 161–64, 178
goldfinch, 5, 187, 236–39
grackle, 40–41, 188
grass nymph butterfly, 121
grasses, 80–82
    flowers of, 80
grasshopper, 5, 15
gray birch tree, 10, 132, 180
gray comma butterfly, 119
gray fox, 209
gray goldenrod, 161, 163
gray tree frog, 67
great blue heron, 91
great horned owl, 2
green frog, 66, 68
greenbottle fly, 23
ground pine tree, 2
grouse, 5
gypsy moth, 23, 171, 219
gypsy moth caterpillar, 219

INDEX

Habenarias (orchids), 94
hag moth caterpillar, 168, 169
harlequin caterpillar, 167
hawk
    feather, 139
    migration, 185
haymaker's mushroom, 144
heart-leaved twayblade, 96
heath aster, 165
hedgehog mushroom, 144
hemlock tree, 216, 233, 234
hepatica, 37–39, 46, 55
hickory horned devil caterpillar, 169
hickory tiger caterpillar, 167
hickory tree, 55, 56, 59
high-bush blackberry, 137
high-bush blueberry, 231
hoary elfin butterfly, 119
holly tree, 189
honeybee, 163
    and asters, 165
hop hornbeam tree, 59, 205–6
hornbeam, 206
horned lark, 5, 8
horned owl, skunk and, 227
house finch, 1, 198
house wren, 187, 188
hummingbird, and jewelweed, 112
Hypholoma mushroom, 144, 145

ice fishing, 222, 223
inch worm, 171
Indian grass, 80
Indian lemonade, 180
insect pests
    and brown thrasher, 190
    dragonflies and, 125–29
    as food for toads, 152
    as food for whippoorwill, 156
    See also insects
insects
    and asters, 165
    as blue jay food, 15
    eggs of, 23
    as food for birds, 26
    as food for ladybugs, 115
    as food for red squirrel, 107
    as food for shrew, 28
    as food for winter birds, 3, 5
    as food for wood frogs, 64
    as food for woodpeckers, 103–4
    and goldenrod, 163
    as hepatica, 38
    and Queen Anne's lace, 140
    and waterlilies, 147
    in winter, 23–27
    See also insect pests *and specific insects*

jack-in-the-pulpit, 69–71
jack-o-lantern mushroom, 144–45
jewelweed, 112–14
junco (bird), 19–22, 187
juniper tree, 233

kingbird, 126
kinglet, 32–34

Labrador tea, 229
ladies' tresses, 178
ladybug, 49–50
    insect pests and, 115
lady's-slipper, 94
lake herring, 220
larch, 233
large-mouthed bass, 220, 222
larvae, 46, 48
    in winter, 23
late purple aster, 166
leopard frog, 64, 66
lesser rattlesnake plantain, 96
Linnaeus, 96
locust borer, 163
Lombardy poplar tree, 8
loon, 153–55

mad-dog skullcap, 85
magnolia tree, 55
maidenhair fern, 188
maple tree, 56
    insect eggs on, 23
    sap of, as food for mourning cloak butterflies, 35, 36
marjoram, 83
masked tricoloma mushroom, 145
mayapple, 34
mayfly nymph, 23
meadow mouse, 5
meadow mushroom, 144
milkweed, 239
milkweed caterpillar, 169, 170
mining bees, 147, 163
mink, 8
mint family, 83–86
moccasin flower, 94
mock-orange shrub, 189
mockernut, 10
mockingbird, 181, 189
mole, distinguished from shrew, 28
monarch butterfly, 120, 121, 164
    migration of, 116
morel mushroom, 145
mosses, 60
moths, 218–19
mourning cloak butterfly, 23, 35–36
    caterpillars of, 170

mouse
  distinguished from shrew, 28
  as food for owls, 7
mushrooms, 144–46
muskrat, 5

nest robbing
  blue jays and, 15
  grackles and, 40
nests
  in backyard, 187–92
  of loon, 155
  of red squirrel, 105
  of sunfish, 90
  of white-footed mouse, 202
New Jersey tea, 228
nightingales, 156
nightshade, 161
Nimble Will (grass), 81
nodding pogonia, 96
nuthatch, 3

oak-loving mushroom, 144
oak tree, 55, 58, 59, 214
  flowers of, 56
old witch grass, 80
orchids, 94–97
Oswego tea, 83
owl, 199–201
owl pellets, 5, 6
  shrew bones in, 30, 31
owlet, 53
oyster mushroom, 145

painted lady butterfly, 119, 123
painted terrapin, 108–10
pale jewelweed, 112
Panaeolus mushroom, 144
partridgeberry, 100, 216
pearl crescent butterfly, 120
peppermint, 83–85
phoebe (bird), 26, 192
Pholiota mushroom, 145
pickerel (fish), 222
pickerel (frog), 66
Pieridae, 122, 124
pike, 222
pileated woodpecker, 14
pine cone, 233
pine flower, 233
pine grosbeak, 183
pine sisken, 8
pine tree, 233–35
pink lady's-slipper, 95
Pipsissewa, 216
pistillate flowers, 55–56, 59
  of hop hornbeam tree, 205
  of sumacs, 180

pistol-case bearer, larvae of, 23
plantain, 96
plants
  as food for shrew, 28
  in winter, 8
  See also specific plants
Pliny, 199, 210
poison sumac, 8
poplar tree, 23, 55
protective coloration, 21
pumpkinseed. *See* sunfish
purple-flowering raspberry, 136
purple love grass, 80
purple skunk cabbage, 2
pussy willow, 84

Queen Anne's lace, 139–40, 166

rabbit. *See* cottontail rabbit
raccoon, 174
ram's head lady's-slipper, 94
raspberry, 134, 136, 137
  See also brambles
red admiral butterfly, 119
red cedar tree, 233
red fox, 208, 209
red maple tree, 55, 59, 180
  flowers of, 56
red oak tree, 180
red osier (plant), 8
red squirrel, 105–7
red-bellied woodpecker, 100
red-humped apple worm caterpillar, 170
redpoll (bird), 5, 8
redwing blackbird, 160, 188
robin, 181, 187
rock bass, 220, 222
rose pogonia, 96
rosemary, 85
rough-stemmed goldenrod, 161
rubus. *See* brambles
ruby-crowned kinglets, 32, 34
ruby-throated hummingbird, 112, 113
rue anemone, 34, 51
ruffed grouse, 2
rufus-sided towhee, 191
Russala mushroom, 145
rusty blackbird, 188

saddleback caterpillar, 168–69
sage, 83
salamander, 210–13
salt-marsh caterpillar, 167
salvia, 85
sassafras, 8, 10, 23
satyr butterfly, 120
scale insects, 15
  ladybugs and, 49

scaly lentinus mushroom, 144
scarlet oak tree, 56, 180
scarlet sage, 85
scarlet-painted cup, 112
scorpion fly, 5
screech owl, 7, 53
serviceberry. *See* shadblow tree
shad fishing, 73
shadblow tree, 72–73
shadbush. *See* shadblow tree
shagbark hickory, 10
sheathed amanitopsis mushroom, 144
shepherd's purse, 178
shrew, 28–30
shrubs, useful, 228–31
   See also specific shrubs
silver maple tree, 55, 59
silver-spotted hesperid butterfly, 119
silverrod, 163
skipper butterfly, 120
skullcap, 83, 85
skunk, 224–27
skunk cabbage, 37, 55, 60, 62
small lady's-slipper, 94
small-mouthed bass, 220, 222
snakes, 98–99, 102
   sense of smell of, 98, 102
   swallowing, 102
   tongues, 98
snow bunting, 5
snowflea, 23–25, 26
snowfly, 23
snowstorms, 3
soldier beetle, 163
Solomon's seal, 161
sparrow, 1
spearmint, 83
spicebush, 228–29, 230
spiders, 193–95
   ballooning, 193, 195
spikelets, 80
spiny oak slug caterpillar, 168, 169
sponge mushroom, 144
spotted jewelweed, 112
spotted purple butterfly, 119
spotted salamander, 210–13
spring, 52–115
   backyard birds in, 187
   flowering tree in, 55–59
   frogs and, 62–63
   harbingers of, 42, 44, 46, 55–59
   juncoes in, 21
spring azure butterfly, 42–43, 45, 119
spring peeper, 61–63, 66
springtail, 5, 23, 147
   See also snowflea
spruce tree, 233
squirrel, 8

staghorn sumac, 180, 181
staminate flowers, 55–56, 59
   of hop hornbeam tree, 205
   of sumacs, 180
starling, 188
stemless lady's-slipper, 94
stonefly, 5, 23, 25, 27
   nymph, 25, 27
sucker (fish), 222
sugar maple tree, 8, 10, 180
   flowering of, 59
sulphur butterfly, 120, 121
sumacs, 180–83
summer tanager, 189
sunfish, 90–93, 222
sunflower, 178, 196–98
sunflower seeds, 198
   chickadees and, 4
survival of the fittest, dandelions and, 77
swallowtail butterfly, 112–13, 119, 121–22, 124
   caterpillar of, 169
swamp white oak tree, 10
sweet bay, 229
sweet fern, 229
sweet gale, 229
sweet goldenrod, 163
sweet lavender, 85
sycamore tree, 10, 59

tadpole, of spring peeper, 62
tall buttercup, 87, 89
tawny emperor butterfly, 119
tea, plants used for, 228–29
ten-petaled sunflower, 196, 198
tent caterpillar, 169, 170
   egg bands of, 23
thimbleberry, 134
thistle, 124
thistle butterfly, 124
Thoreau, Henry David, 130, 178, 199
thyme, 83
tiger moth, 167
tiger swallowtail butterfly, 120, 122
   caterpillar of, 169
toad, 150–52
   food for, 152
   myths about, 150
   poisonous fluid of, 150
toadstools. *See* mushrooms
Torrey, Bradford, 236
tortoiseshell butterfly, 119
towhee, 190
tracks
   of bobcat, 12, 14
   of shrew, 28
trailing arbutus, 34, 97
tree sparrow, 3, 5, 187

trees
  autumn colors, 180
  flowering of, 55–59
  growth rings, 76
  identification of, 8, 10
  and insect eggs, 23
  stumps, 60
  in winter, 8–11
  See also specific trees
trout. *See* brook trout
trout lily, 230
true orchids, 94
trumpet, 112
tufted titmouse, 188
tulip tree, 2, 8
tupelo, 10
turtles, 108–11
tussock moth, 23
tuxedo. *See* swallowtail butterfly
twayblade, 96

Vedalia beetle, 49
veery nest, 71
vermilion mushroom, 144
violet-tip butterfly. *See* tortoiseshell butterfly
violet, 51
Vorticella, 8

wanderer butterfly, 119
water flea, 8
water plants, 5
water strider, 147
waterlilies, 147–49
waxy accaria mushroom, 144
webs, of caterpillars, 169–70
webworm tents, 171
whippoorwill, 156–57
whirligig beetle, 147
white birch, 130, 132
white cabbage butterfly, 119
white-breasted nuthatch, 187
white-crowned sparrow, 187–88
white-footed mouse, 202–4
white-fringed orchid, 94, 96
white lady's-slipper, 94
white oak tree, 8
white pine tree, 235
white-tailed deer, 11, 234
white-tailed dragonfly, 126
white-throated sparrow, 187–88
white waterlily, 147–48
whitefish, 220
Whitman, Walt, 80, 137

whorled pogonia, 96, 97
wild black cherry, 8
wild calla lily, 149
wild carrot. *See* Queen Anne's lace
wild columbine, 51
wild red raspberry, 136
wild rice, 80
wild strawberry, 89
wild turkey, 2, 62, 107, 217
  and wild blueberry, 232
wildflowers, 47, 51
  in winter, 37–39
  See also specific wildflowers
willow, 56
wineberry, 134
winter landscape, 8–11
winter maple tree, 11
winter, 1–50
  animals in, 8
  backyard birds in, 187
  birds in, 1–2, 3–5, 6, 7, 8, 15–22, 40–41
  freshwater fish in, 220–22
  goldfinch in, 236, 237, 239
  insects in, 23–27
  moths in, 218
  mourning cloak butterfly in, 35–36
  plants in, 8
  trees in, 8–11
  wildflowers in, 37–39
wintergreen, 60
  berries of, 100
wood anemone, 34
wood-boring beetles, 15
wood frog, 62, 64, 65, 66
wood nymph butterfly, 120
woodpecker, 1, 2, 5, 103–4
wooly bear caterpillar, 167, 168
worker bee, 48
worm, 8

yellow bear caterpillar, 167, 171
yellow birch tree, 132
yellow bullhead lily, 148
yellow lady's-slipper, 94
yellow perch, 220, 222, 223
yellow sulphur butterfly, 119
yellow waterlily, 147
yellow willow tree, 8, 10
yellow-fringed orchid, 96
yellow-rumped warbler, 194
yew tree, 233

zigzag goldenrod, 161